UNCORKING WINE

OPERATING INSTRUCTIONS FOR WINE ENJOYMENT

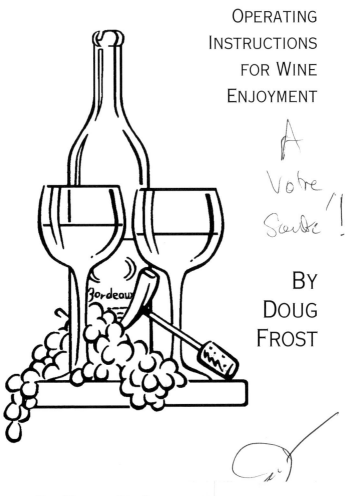

À
votre
Santé!

BY DOUG FROST

THE WRITERS CO., F

D1112002

UNCORKING WINE
Copyright © 1996 by The Writer's Co.

All rights reserved. No part of this book may be reproduced in any manner
without the express written consent of the publisher, except in the
case of brief excerpts in reviews and articles.

ISBN 0-9653177-0-6

Library of Congress Catalog Card Number 96-060723

Printed in the U.S.A. by Constable-Hodgins Printing Co., Inc.

The Writer's Company
2510 Grand Boulevard, Suite 504
Kansas City, Missouri 64108
(816) 221-7006

First Edition

WHAT I LIKE ABOUT WINE

All the questions I have answered here have been asked of me at some or other time. To me they represent the honest utilization of an honest beverage and what I love most about the people who often ask questions is that they are free from pretention and posturing.

Truthfully, most of these questions were offered by blushing neophytes that felt, being born without the answers, somehow inadequate. No matter what else I have gotten done with this or other works on wine in my life, I hope that I usually managed to answer their questions without adding to that sense of inadequacy.

All that is necessary to enjoy wine is a nose, a mouth, a stomach (a few other organs) and, hopefully, a few friends. Describing wine and its minutiae is as unimportant to enjoying wine as is being able to quote the Hite report during sex.

Enough writers have tried to mediate our love of wine with their oh-so-specific terminology and rules. I have no such intention, but ask that you enjoy it any damn way you please.

Doug Frost
April 1996

TABLE OF CONTENTS

ACKNOWLEDGEMENTS

Amberlight Photography
Wilson Daniels, Ltd.
Frederick Wildman & Sons
Dave Fisher – Art Production
Mark Huebner – Drawings
Nate Fors – Maps
Payson W. Lowell, Constable-Hodgins Printing Co., Inc.

THE STRAIGHT JUICE

What is a varietal?

Put technically, a varietal is a subtype of a species of grapevine, with names like Chardonnay and Cabernet Sauvignon being used to describe the vine, the grapes and the wine resulting from them.

Less technically, New World (America, Australia, etc.) wines are labeled varietally, with the producer as the brand, e.g., Mondavi Cabernet Sauvignon or Beringer Chardonnay. The Old World (read: Europe) has usually bottled its wines by vineyard or area name.

Both New and Old Worlds therefore have paradigms that they focus upon. In the Old European Tradition a wine had to taste like its good neighbor to be legitimate. Lacking traditions, most New World wines are fashioned according to a perceived notion of how a particular varietal should taste. So Chardonnay producers always make certain that their Chardonnay smells and tastes like it has been aged in expensive French oak barrels, even if it hasn't.

In America, a bottle of Chardonnay (or any other varietal) should have at least 75% of that particular grape in the bottle. Though this provides some truth-in-labeling guarantees, the rule has hindered forward progress in wine blending as only 25% of other grapes are allowed. Still for most consumers, the varietal gives a quick indication of the character of a given wine and so the practice of varietal-labeling has been a big factor in the explosion of wine sales.

The New World's infatuation with varietals dates back to the 1960's when Robert Mondavi, among others, explored the grapes in great use in France and concluded that these particular grapes were the reason for French wine successes.

In the Old World, varietal bottlings are much less prevalent. One thousand years of winegrowing has created a confusion of grapes and, until the Americans arrived, many growers weren't sure what some vines were actually called.

Only later did it become apparent that much European success was based upon blending of different grapes. In Bordeaux, few bottlings are more than 55% of any one grape, and some producers swear that the 2% Petite Verdot (a taut-tasting varietal) that they utilize, is imperative to the wine's excellence.

We can expect blends to become more important in the New World as winemakers are excited by the quality and styles acheived. Less enthusiastic are the marketers, who prefer the simplicity of varietal labels.

How is wine made?

Wine is very, very simple stuff to make; that's why it was surely mankind's first alcoholic beverage. You take grapes, squash them (though even that stage is somewhat unnecessary), put them in a container, cover them and leave them alone for a few days. The yeast that live on the grapes begin the process, converting the natural grape sugars to alcohol.

The science of winemaking lies in measuring the many, many chemical transformations that occur in that seemingly simple process, and in controlling the rate and temperature of fermentation.

The art of winemaking lives in the tasting and assessment of the wine as it comes into being, and in choosing the influences upon the wine. These influences include the temperature of fermentation and storage, the size and material of the fermenting and storing vessels, the length of time for each, and the selection of constituent grapes, vineyards and lots of the final blend.

Believe it or not, that's it. And you could read hundreds of books that detail the ramifications of each of these decisions.

How are wines labeled?

Naming a wine is not as simple as it sounds. The name of the wine is usually either the varietal (or variety of grapevine) or the place (the name of a town or a vineyard area). Most New World wines are named after the varietal (e.g. Chardonnay, Cabernet Sauvignon, Merlot, et.al.) and many if not most Old World wines are named after the place from which they come.

As simple as this sounds, things get obtuse from here. In France, wines are almost always named after the place, but which place? Let's propose that the wine comes from a little chateau in Bordeaux called Chateau La Fleur Milon, right next door to Chateau Lafite Rothschild. The wine made there could be called Bordeaux, Medoc, Pauillac or Chateau La Fleur Milon.

That is, the wine might be named after the region from which it comes (Bordeaux), the sub-region of Bordeaux (Medoc), the commune (Pauillac) or the specific chateau. But in addition to any chateau name, French wines also carry a title called an appellation. "Appellation" is the French term for the wine's region of origin, and this origin can be rather generic (such as "Bordeaux") or very specific (such as "Pauillac").

In truth, Chateau La Fleur Milon is sold as Chateau La Fleur Milon and carries an appellation of "Bordeaux". The wine made next door at Chateau Lafite carries an appellation of "Pauillac".

In these instances, the label and the appellation have become more specific. The inference in all French wine is, that the more specific the label, the better the wine. If a chateau sells its wine to a large concern, to be integrated into a blend called Bordeaux or Pauillac, chances are that the grower at the chateau is not terrifically concerned about the quality of the wine, just that the grapes are ripe.

If a grower is placing his or her name upon the bottle, with the name of their chateau upon it, chances are good (but not great) that the producer has taken greater care to protect the chateau's reputation. In truth, all a chateau has of value is its reputation and the quality of its existing wine.

This is as true in Bordeaux as in Burgundy or the Rhone. Bourgogne (as generic Burgundy is called) is not likely to be as good as a seperate vineyard area, such as Gevrey Chambertin. And Gevrey Chambertin Premier Cru Les Cazetiers is likely to be better wine than straight Gevrey, though not as good as Le Chambertin, the small vineyard for which all vineyards in the area are named.

Two areas in France are exceptions; some wines from the Languedoc are named after the varietal, as they are destined for grocery store shelves in America and elsewhere. And in Alsace, next door to Germany, most wines are named varietally; Riesling, Gewurztraminer or Pinot Blanc, to cite the most common.

Germany always names the wine after the area, whether from an enormous region such as the Rhein vineyards where Liebfraumilch is produced, or the tiny steepness of the hill that comprises Piesporter Goldtroepfchen.

Italy's wines are labeled pretty much anyway they please, which gives insight into the way Italians approach wine laws.

In the New World, few wines are labeled by any name other than the grape and the producer. Thus, one might see Robert Mondavi Chardonnay (from Napa Valley) or Rosemount Merlot (from Australia) or even Villiera Fume Blanc (from South Africa). But this simplistic approach belies a sticky problem; how much of the wine in the bottle is Chardonnay, Merlot or Fume Blanc?

In America, the law stipulates that any bottle labeled varietally must contain at least 75% of the varietal listed on the bottle. Thus Pine Ridge Cabernet Sauvignon Rutherford is 81% Cabernet Sauvignon, 9% Merlot and 10% Cabernet Franc..

But prior to 1983, the law only stipulated 50% minimum for the varietal listed. So since 1973 Phelps Insignia has had only 65% Cabernet Sauvignon or so in it; not coincidentally, Insignia was the first Bordeaux-styled blend in California, as Phelps prefers an aesthetically pleasing blend to an arbitrarily-determined percentage such as 75%.

So some wines today are produced in America which have no varietals and many of them go by the curious name of meritage wines.

What are Meritage wines?

Glad you asked. The Meritage Association is a group of American wine producers who were unhappy with the 75% rule and who coined the term "meritage" to designate wines that are composed of Bordeaux-style blends. Thus a red meritage wine must have at least two of the classic Bordeaux grapes in it (Cabernet Sauvignon, Cabernet Franc, Merlot, Malbec and Petit Verdot) and a white meritage is made of Sauvignon Blanc, Semillon and, technically, Muscadelle, though I'm not aware of much use of that obscure grape.

The term Meritage is a rather odd term; it's never pronounced correctly (*Mer*itage not meri*tage*), though quibbling about the pronounciation of an invented word is a niggling complaint indeed.

The word was the result of a six month search in 1983 and 1984 for a term to replace those then in use; Proprietary Red, Red Table Wine or Bordeaux-Style Blend. Gee, I thought Reserve might work pretty well, but then we squandered that word on less noble wines.

The word itself was chosen by a panel of representatives of each of the forty-three charter members of the Meritage Association. Nearly any time I see the word I have to think upon a sweet but slow participant who was part of the panel. Asked by her fellow winery employees of the results of the nationwide search, she replied, "Oh, you guys are going to love this name." "What is it?", they pressed. "Well, I don't remember, but you guys are going to love it."

That limns my complaint about the word. It's made-up, it really doesn't mean anything, so how can anyone remember it?

For all my complaints, one of the rules surrounding the use of the term "Meritage", has made an undoubtable improvement in American wine. This rule stipulated that a Meritage wine be one of the two most expensive wines from the participant winery. Roughly speaking, this means that an experiment in blending was promoted to a flagship for each winery.

I love the idea that an experiment, albeit a well-selected and closely-guided experiment, could be rewarded and scrutinized by the market like this. In my labor force days, we called this 'incentive'. Without question, many wineries, such as Guenoc, Dalla Valle, and Flora Springs have produced delicious to great wines under the influence of Meritage. I remain convinced that many of them would not have had as many successes without it.

That said, the term Meritage will probably be a footnote in the wine books ten years on.

Is Reserve Wine better than regular wine?

It ought to be but isn't. Jess Jackson of Kendall Jackson should take some responsibility for eviscerating the word of its meaning. In some countries, such as Portugal, there are legal definitions for Reserve wines. But in the hands of Jackson and many others, there is no "there" there.

Every wine Kendall Jackson makes is called 'Reserve' something. The standard line of wines is called Vintner's Reserve and the true reserve wines are called Proprietor's Reserve. Annoyingly, Jackson's ploy has worked (aided by excellent marketing and skillful, if sometimes commercial, winemaking). Kendall Jackson wines are more popular than any other line of wines in their price range.

Others should shoulder some of the credit, chief among them is Glen Ellen. But it is best to ignore the word "reserve" on a

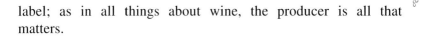

label; as in all things about wine, the producer is all that matters.

Why are some wines aged in wood barrels?

The symbiosis between wood barrels and wine was first noticed by the Romans. The Celts invented the modern barrel, utilizing iron hoops and producing barrels for transport of many goods, not the least of them wine. Happily oak barrels added character to wine and so their use has always been widespread in Europe. Though woods from chestnut to redwood have been used (and still are in use) the wood of choice has always been oak, in fact, oak trees also supply the bark used to cut corks for closures.

Barrels have several effects on wine; one is that the wines are exposed to small amounts of air as they lie in the barrel, through the air trapped inside the barrel and lurking between the staves, and the air invading whenever the bung is removed to check the wine or replace any wine lost through evaporation. If the wine were already in bottle or locked inside a stainless steel tank, the influence of air would be tremendously diminished. This controlled aeration relaxes the wine, fattening it and aging it.

Oak barrels also impart the flavor of oak (the other woods are neutral—unless you count *rauli*, a wretched Chilean barrel wood, best used for warmth on a cold Andean night). Oak can greatly alter the taste of a wine, dependent upon how large the barrel is, how the barrel was coopered, how new and at what point and for what period of time, the wine is held in it.

These are all decisions on the winemaker's recipe card and seemingly small choices can yield radically-influenced wines. For a time, American winemakers believed that new oak meant quality wine. Thankfully, some of the smarter producers are remembering that wine should smell like grapes first and oak last.

Are French oak barrels the best?

There are plenty of reasons to argue for that position. All Bordeaux (great Cabernet, Merlot and Sauvignon Blanc), Burgundy

(Chardonnay or Pinot Noir), and some Rhone wines (Syrah and many other varietals), are partially about the flavors of French oak. These winemakers would rather shoot their relatives than waste their wines on neutral and boring Yugoslavian or German oaks or submit their precious juice to the vulgarity of an American oak barrel. Truthfully, the great Bordeaux produced between the World Wars were aged most often in American oak. And prior to World War I, most Bordeaux were aged in Yugoslavian oak. Be prepared for a fist-fight if you try to tell that to a contemporary French vigneron.

Most oak barrels are very neutral, these include those made from Italian, Portuguese, Spanish, Yugoslavian and other Eastern European oaks. At the opposite extreme, American oaks tend to be highly-flavored and remind some people of vanilla, coconut, saw-dust, even dill pickles. Don't laugh, it's true. The Australians are fond of this flavor and they have coopered American oak by clas-sic French methods to produce barrels that are intensely-flavored but delightful for use with white or red wines.

French oak is smoky and less obtrusive. Part of this difference is due to coopering methods, partly due to the climatic conditions of central and southern France. For me, there is no other barrel for Chardonnay than a French oak barrel.

For red wines, the possibilities are less proscribed. Oaks from Missouri, Kentucky and north to Minnesota are excellent when they are coopered for wine and not whiskey. Oregon has shown promise with its oaks, which seem less, well, American.

How does somebody make a great wine?

Terroir, yield, climat, blends; these are the whipping sticks of those that want to argue the origin of great wines. Each term holds within its grain of sand a world of possibility and argument.

Terroir and climat are two roughly-equal French terms for vine-yard areas. The European (read: historic) way to describe a wine was by its place of origin and the closer one could limn this place, the better. Thus vineyards that could distinguish themselves could be better rewarded. Burgundy, the world's most closely-defined vineyard area, is often defined by its denizens in these terms.

A climat is a vineyard and, at its best, a homogenous vineyard area. For a Burgundian, there may be fifty climats within a defined vineyard. Even a "clos", or walled vineyard, such as Clos de Vougeot, has nearly as many co-owners. Any of them may see the vineyard as containing many, many climats.

Terroir is a description of the manner by which a climat expresses itself. A climat is a defined place with boundaries. Terroir is the presence of the place in the grape and in the resultant wine. If it sounds mystical and New Age, I can't help that. The French, who are otherwise very practical people, get all gooey-eyed when contemplating minor issues of language, especially their own.

Yields are much discussed by wine writers. Though I love to differ from them, there is no arguing yield's importance. It's simply not possible to make great wine with high yields. The world's greatest wines are the result of agonizingly small yields, which justifies, in some measure, the high prices these wines command.

Yet, most of our wine (at least 99.9% of it) is nothing like great. It is, however, increasingly good. This improvement happens in the face of increased yields in many vineyards in California, the Pacific Northwest, Australia, southern France, northern Italy and northern Spain and New Zealand. Improvements in vineyard management here have led to increases in both yield and quality.

If greatness is on a winemaker's mind, he or she is going to severely curtail the yield. Good wine can be produced at eight tons of grapes per acre of vines. So-so wines probably occur above that. Great wines are almost always less than three tons per acre. Imagine that a vine has only so much flavor to give, and it can either be diluted among many bunches of grapes or concentrated in a few.

If yield were all that was required of great wines, there would be great wines in 47 states. Instead, *an exceptional terroir must be married with great grape varietals in small yields to make great wine* and, often, the blend of differing varietals holds the final key.

Though this concept has been less than sexy for some time, the idea of the blend is gaining cache' in California, where only a few years ago the winemaker (actually just a small number of well-known winemakers) was seen as auteur in a nearly-blank medium waiting for his/her signature.

Lately many believe that the mere presence of a blend of grapes may be enough to propell a wine into greatness; this is the origin of the term and concept of "Meritage" wines.

I am utterly convinced that blending of grapes, styles and clones (subtypes of varietals) and, most importantly, vineyards, is our best resource for the future production of "good" wines throughout the world. Great wine, however, is not a blend of differing places and vineyards; it comes from one vineyard of character and substance.

Most knowledgeable people argue now that wine is "made in the vineyard" but the men and women on the tractors are too poorly paid to be heroes in America.

Instead the wisdom of some owner in owning the right piece of land is preeminent in the wine marketplace. Defining these places is less tricky than I have described it above. All winemakers and winedrinkers are looking for the twin goals of drama and balance.

That much is clear. Less clear is our definition of these goals. Australia's wines are by origin very dramatic, rich and showy wines. Whether they are well-balanced enough to age well is an issue worth debating at this time.

California's reds are by birth rich, warm and tannic. Excellence here depends upon a winegrower and winemaker's ability to ameliorate these characteristics. A grower here is looking for as long a growing season as possible. Ripeness is easy to come by here, less so is balance.

Most classic European wine regions are much cooler than California and Australia, so ripeness is hard to achieve. To the French, greatness is ripeness, but not to a Californian. A California wine-maker wants balance and the best wines the Californian receives from their favorite vineyard may lack it.

Instead, a blend of vineyard properties may be the panacea in these warmer climes. Not surprisingly, the blending of varietals is most common in the warmest parts of France.

How is a cork made?

A cork is generally a natural cylinder cut from the bark of a twenty-five year or older cork oak in Portugal, Spain or northern Africa. Most Champagne corks are composed of three pieces of cork glued together. Some corks are made from cork particles glued together and called composite corks.

The newest cork is synthetic and goes by names like Cellucork or Supremecork. Many winemakers are terrified by them and insist that they taint or spoil the wine they seal. I think that the afore-mentioned winemakers are really, really paranoid. I don't find a trace of taint and think that Gallo should adopt them immediately for all their cork-finished wines (let the big boys do the expensive experimentation). Certainly they are proven as flawless closures for short-term drinking wines.

Not so for standard oak corks. "Corkiness", as it is called, reveals its origin eponymously, in that TCA (trichloroanisole) breeds in the microscopic valleys of a cork in the presence of trace amounts of chlorine. This aromatic taint ruins a wine quickly and forever, rendering any great wine only barely drinkable (More's the mockery. Why doesn't it just destroy the wines altogether?).

Solving TCA seemed simple, discontinue using chlorine to bleach corks for cosmetic purposes. Trouble is, there's enough chlorine in our atmosphere to trigger TCA growth.

Estimates of TCA contamination in today's corks range from 5% to 20%. The lower estimate is closer I suspect. Still, do you like knowing the fifty of your one thousand bottles are a waste of money and cellar space? Break 'em now.

Tightened testing is now the standard. But there are still up to 10% of all corks growing vile aromas. The cork industry will act when it has to (fiscally) and so you should enthusiastically embrace the new synthetic cellular corks, Cellucork and Supreme Cork, both very American products.

Both cork companies produce excellent products, with tremendous strength and integrity (like, they don't break or tear.) They're still young to be sure, but they are likely to be very firm closures in twenty and thirty years when your natural corks are turning into something closely resembling sand in the shape of a cork.

But synthetic corks are untested for longevity. We need another ten years to be sure, though the good record of the last five years is likely to change the general attitude. While probably 50% of all California winemakers today think synthetic corks are dangerous and can taint a wine, that number will change quickly over the next ten years as corked wines become too embarassing to tolerate.

The best houses (Lafite, Mouton and others similar) have acheived nearly 100% integrity of their corks, all but a few free of TCA taint. It can be done. The natural cork is not gone, but the cork industry has to change.

How important is the vintage?

There is a rule in winedom that the producer is more important than anything, especially the vintage. Simply put, a great producer does everything possible to make great wine, regardless of the reason, but a bad producer makes bad wine, no matter how great the vintage.

To understand why this is so, we can look at many aspects in viticulture and vinification, but two issues ring supreme to me: site and yield.

The grower has a plethora of choices when selecting site—with issues of topography, elevation, aspect, trellising, varietals, vine density, and soil diversity only a part of the dilemma. To a great degree, site can ameliorate the difficulties of a vintage. In 1994, a number of excellent Bordeaux were produced by the top estates,

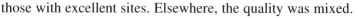

those with excellent sites. Elsewhere, the quality was mixed.

Yield is a controversial subject now but I remain convinced that the best wines are made by selecting the best grapes. I hope that's not too radical a concept.

Those growers that include every available grape in their crush make less good a wine than those that are picky about their grapes. And those that control the rate of growth of the vine in order to keep their yields low are making better wine.

WINE AND GOOD BODY

Are there additives in wine?

Additives in wine are few and happily far between. Most wine is the result of natural products; grape juice, some sort of container, and yeast, and yeast is often naturally-occuring in the vineyard.

Yeast are more often innoculated into the grape juice, but these yeast are still natural, living organisms. Some winemakers add vitamin C to assist the yeast in growing rapidly but I would hope that you could concur that that is a pretty benign additive.

Once the yeast have concluded their work, the wine needs to be protected from the harmful effects of oxygen. Small doses of elemental sulfur are the tool of choice for the last three hundred and fifty years in winemaking.

The trace amounts of this natural mineral are usually between twenty and fifty parts per million, far less than one finds in a salad bar. Some severe asthmatics have experienced bad reactions to such modest proportions.

Another stabilizer used most frequently in bulk wines is potassium sorbate. Less is known about this additive and I see no good reason to use it, as it might carry some uncertain side effects, and as its use is redundant with the availability of sulfur.

Finally, certain compounds are added to wines, which are then removed from the wine prior to bottling. These fining agents, used to remove dead yeast cells and any other recalcitrant particles to clarify the wines include bentonite (basically, clay), isinglass (basically, pureed fish), diatemaceous earth (more clay) and egg whites. A few decades ago animal blood was pretty popular but that doesn't go down so well anymore.

I repeat, all of these compounds are removed from the wines before bottling.

What are sulfites?

As described above, natural sulfur is used to protect wine from oxygen—it bonds with oxygen to remove available and damaging air from any wine container, especially a bottle.

Its purpose and effects (or lack thereof) are well-documented and sulfur is controversial only in the good ol' US of A.

Sulfur is a natural mineral extracted from the earth, which is why Europeans consider organic wines to include those that have been treated with sulfur. In America, we know better. Here our organic wine producers eschew the use of trace amounts of sulfur and tend to offer lightly-colored, bland wines as a result. I guess we showed them.

Sulfur became an issue in the mid-80's when a handful of severe asthmatics had dangerous reactions to the salad bars so popular then. Aesthetic considerations aside, these asthmatics had plenty to react against; most salad bars utilized levels of sulfur over two hundred parts per million. Levels at half that make wine undrinkable.

Though most wines carry levels around forty-five parts per million, wine was immediately targeted as a dangerous element in society. The mis-guided CSPI (Center for Science in the Public Interest) led a successful campaign to require all wines to carry warning labels, the famous "CONTAINS SULFITES" one sees on wine bottles today.

With hundreds of years of healthy experience, we should not concern ourselves with minor levels of sulfur. Less certain is the presence of sorbates, which have not yet be shown to be troublesome but which are extremely new.

A misinformed public still wonders about sulfites. If you are severely asthmatic, avoid sulfured wines. Avoid even more grocery store fruit and salad bars, and especially, dried fruits. These are far more dangerous. Is anyone from CSPI listening?

Why am I allergic to red wine?

The issue of allergies and wine is still a mystery. Several years ago, we thought that histamines, much higher in red wines than in whites, were to blame for the well-known quandry of red wine headaches or allergy attacks.

The best I can say is to tell you that that theory has been completely debunked. The newest and most promising line of inquiry is a group of compounds called tyramines, present in red wines and in blue cheeses. These seem to produce rapid headaches in certain sufferers and new research is gaining as fast as low funding will allow.

That said, I have heard hundreds of stories about this or that person's own problems with wine, or spirits, or alcohol. There is little difference between red wine and white wine or between beer and spirits for that matter, so I'm unsure why people have such different reactions to these beverages. I think that much of this is psychosomatic, frankly, though that doesn't stop a sufferer from suffering. It just makes it harder to solve.

Why does Champagne give such fierce hangovers?

This is an easy one. The myth that the bubbles in Champagne, or sparkling wines, speeds the alcohol to the bloodstream is entertainingly silly. If the bloodstream were filled with CO_2 bubbles by consuming Champagne, the most common effect of drinking it would be sudden death.

Instead the real headache with sparkling wines is that they are consumed too liberally. Trust me, I spent years as a banquet manager. If I was doing a party of one hundred and they were drinking red wine, a case of twelve bottles was sufficient. If white wine were used three cases would be needed, but if sparkling wine were served, four or more cases would be consumed easily.

Because sparkling wine tastes as rich and frothy as adult soda pop, it's generally consumed like it's soda pop.

Certainly, wines which have some residual sugar to them seem to exacerbate hangover intensity. And, surprisingly, sparklers, even great Champagnes, have a touch of sweetness to them. Because the CO_2 bubbles create the sensation of dryness, for a sparkling wine to taste balanced, it needs to have around 1% residual sugar or more.

Sugar, though, is not the culprit. Sparkling wines are easy to drink and those who are inexperienced usually end up drinking too much.

Is red wine healthy?

I like to think so, but then I drink a lot of it. Many of the healthy effects of red wine consumption have been substantiated through demographic studies, with wide populations in the US and abroad, and in smaller, more-focused studies. Demographically speaking, the people who drink red wine are often educated and more likely to take care of themselves. Therefore, the fact that they drink red wine is coincident with longer, healthier lives.

Still, I am convinced that it is much more than coincidence. Certainly, scientists have identified two important substances, resveratrol and quercetin, as extremely benficial substances. These compounds have been shown to reduce platelet buildup in blood vessels and reduce incidence of stroke and heart disease. Moderate consumption of wine can alter the ratio of HDL cholesterol to LDL cholesterol, thus reducing the bad LDL's in favor of more beneficial HDL's.

Resveratol, quercetin, and alcohol in general and wine in particular behave as anti-oxidants, which may explain their mechanism for reducing stroke and heart disease in dramatic studies in America and Europe.

Naturally, science is at work isolating those compounds so they can package them into little pills for people. We wouldn't want to enjoy the benefits of these and have fun drinking too, would we? America is nothing if not a Puritanical society.

As well, I would argue that isolating a few ingredients is not good science. These active ingredients are healthful, but it is most likely that they are best in concert with the other myriad active and inactive ingredients in wine.

I still will argue that the Mediterranean diet is healthful for reasons more than the particular ingredients, be they red wine and olive oil or whatever. Try the Mediterranean lifestyle of long, happy lunches, fresh vegetables and fruits, lots of seafood and little red meat, fats in proportion to other good substances, happy dinners, consistent drinking and little or no binge drinking with lots of walking.

BEING AT HOME WITH WINE

How should you store wine?

The rules of wine storage are simple; the darker, the colder, the less movement, the better. There is no doubt that any temperature over seventy degrees Fahrenheit ages wines quickly. More importantly, any temperature over eighty degrees damages wines irreparably. If that temperature seems unlikely to you, check that wine rack in your kitchen.

Wines should stay in the basement until they're served. If you don't have a basement then at least keep the wines in the dark; as perhaps you should do with your children or roommates. Light is the enemy of wine as much as it is for beer; keep your wines protected from light, both natural and artificial, whenever possible.

Humidity is less definitive an issue. Though it's not terrifically necessary that the area be above 80% relative humidity, it's also true that very dry conditions can compromise the good condition of the cork. A cork is an imperfect closure, one that is well-designed to last twenty to thirty years. But if the temperature in the cellar fluctuates greatly the cork is bound to lose its necessary elasticity.

Cork is also compromised by shipping, especially if the bottle is older. Ship and transport wines as little as possible because, if an older bottle has been moved a number of times, the cork can be soft or even broken up.

The wine, surprisingly, may still be sound. Not long ago I conducted a vertical tasting of Petrus, and one bottle, the 1964, was delivered by the owner the day before the tasting. In the cellar it was fine, but the movement of the car caused the cork to slip into the neck of the bottle. There it hung by a slender molecule of cork waiting for me to open it.

At opening I had no illusions about the anticipated quality of the wine; but the show must go on and all that. It turns out the 1964 was the best bottle of the evening. As one will say often of wine, go figure.

How do you start a cellar?

Perhaps the more important question is, why do you start a cellar? In ages past, a cellar was an inheritance handed down from generation to generation; the keys passed from one old cobweb-laden aristocrat to another, younger, less-cobweb-laden aristocrat.

Today, those collecting wine are as likely to be middle-class as aristo and the cellar is meant for tomorrow, not some decade far away. Most cellars are expected to serve several purposes; to keep great wines for distant and future consumption, to allow young wines to gain a softening amount of age and to store excellent wines for current consumption with friends and family.

I think that it's imperative to know precisely what proportions a cellar owner needs in order to satisfy these very different needs.

Make a decision in advance as to how much of each you need and how much you're willing to spend to get it.

Once you have determined your various purposes for the cellar, accept that different criteria exist for each category. If you are only slightly knowledgeable about wine and if you find something you like, buy it and drink it as much as you like. Enjoy it and get to know it; you might find that it doesn't age as well as you expected. Truthfully, many very tasty wines are meant to be enjoyed early in their lives and are not likely to gain in character and may even diminish.

That doesn't mean you don't buy them; I repeat, buy them and drink them happily.

The wines that you buy to age in your cellar briefly are those wines about which you are learning. Some will improve, some may not; don't worry about it, drink and be content.

Wines for long-term cellaring are a completely different matter. If I have learned nothing else in my own cellaring, it is to buy and keep only the best. Buy the absolute best wines you can, because you are investing more than money. You are investing time and hope. There is nothing worse than pulling a wine from the cellar, a wine that you have saved for years, to find that it's pretty damn boring. That hurts.

Avoid pain. Buy the best. Which brings us to the next question....

How do you know when a wine is ready to drink?

Wine is a very unpredictable beverage with only intelligent experience and imperfect intuition to guide one in assessing the durability of any bottle. The best method is to buy enough bottles to taste any wine frequently, watching them as they mature. But, aside from buying wine in twelve case lots, how is a normal person to guesstimate a wine's maturity?

As experience and intuition are the best tool, ask or read someone knowledgeable on the particular wine. If the wine is American, call the winery and ask them. Most often you'll get patched to someone in the tasting room, but about half of the time that person has a clue. I hasten to point out that that's a far better percentage than most retail stores can offer.

Robert Parker has a method that he admits is inconsistent at best, though he uses it, and I have always taken it as strong evidence. After opening and tasting a bottle, he recorks the wine and tastes it the next day. If it still tastes good, it may age well for several years, even ten. If it ages well for two days, perhaps five to fifteen years. Three days, ten to twenty years. Four days, who knows?

I paraphrase Parker's system, but you get the drift.

What is tannin? Alternately, why are some red wines so bitter?

As outlined in food and wine (see page 33), tannin is a con-stituent element of wine that aids in a wine's longevity as well as allowing the wine to combine well with food. As well, tannin begins to link up with anthocyanin (or coloring material) as a wine ages. As these molecules link up they become gross (or large) and drop to the bottom of the bottle. That material is called sediment. Theoretically, when one sees sediment in a wine it has aged enough to have lost most of its tannins and is probably ready to drink.

Is sediment good?

The sedimentary deposit in red wine most often appears after the wine is fully mature. Some iconoclastic and dedicated wine-makers bottle without any filtration and these wines may leave a sludgy deposit on the bottle within the first few years after pur-chase.

Sedimental deposit can arise from several sources; it may be tar-taric acid, the predominant acid in grapes, mixed with coloring matter, or it may be tannin and coloring matter, or anthocyanins, that have bonded together and precipitated to the bottom of the bottle. As this process has occured, the wine has become softer and less tannic, it has also become lighter in color, as tannin and antho-cyanins have turned into tiny sandy particles. Concurrently, dark-ly-colored wines have more anthocyanins to shed and more sedi-ment at maturity. Light-colored grapes such as Pinot Noir rarely have much sediment.

When you see sediment building up in the bottom of the bottle, the wine is exhibiting its complete maturity and may need drink-ing. Certainly fine sediment is a sign of good storage. As well, it's important to transport the wine carefully so that the well-stored bottle doesn't become cloudy. It's necessary to decant a mature bottle so you and your friends don't have to filter the sludge with your teeth.

Pour the wine gently into a very clean glass decanter and watch the neck and shoulder of the bottle for chunks of sediment. Stop pouring when the fine sand is beginning to enter the neck of the bottle. Later when you are desperate for more of your great bottle, use cheesecloth to strain the sediment. Coffee filters, often suggested by clerks and wine writers, use chemical adhesives to hold their fibers together and leave a residual taste.

Is there glass in the bottom of my German wine?

Cold, northerly vineyards such as Germany's tend to produce wines very high in acidity. As the predominant grape acid is tartaric acid, this is found in spades in German wines. Most wine producers throughout the world chill their wines for a few weeks to near freezing before bottling. This process, called cold stabilization, turns excess tartaric acid into crystals which can be left out of the bottled wine.

Some wines are not cold-stabilized for reasons that range from laziness to incompetence to a sense that cold-stabilization reduces some of the quality of a great wine. These wines will, upon refrigeration, show more crystals in the bottle, either stuck to the cork or in the bottom of the glass. The crystals are harmless, tasteless, odorless and, if you collect enough of them, you could sell them to your grocer as cream of tartar, a common thickening agent in cooking. Good luck.

Why do some people chill their Beaujolais?

I am reminded of the warning on the sides of Cold Duck bottles, "serve well chilled." In other words, if you get this stuff cold enough, you won't notice how miserable it tastes. Ditto for most American beers.

Beaujolais Nouveaux in particular is indifferent enough wine to need a decent chilling to add some pleasure. Most straight-forward Beaujolais is about fruit and little else, so a slight chill will increase the fruitiness and the enjoyment.

Colder temperatures tend to emphasize the acid constituents of wine, fruit acids as well as tannic acid. Thus a slight chilling will give a fruitier but tarter wine. A tannic young monster is even more monstrous when it is cold out of the barrel and the tannins are swirling in cool anticipation of your tender mouth.

Concurrently, warmer temperatures emphasize the alcohol. Thus a light, insipid wine can be made to taste more substantial when it is not cool, but is room temperature. It depends upon what you're drinking and on what you want.

What is room temperature and should I serve all red wines at that temperature?

I wish I knew where the old room-temperature phrase originated. All wine is meant to be served cool, say, at around sixty-five degrees. There is nothing more unpleasant than a red wine served at room temperature in the middle of August. At these times I think fondly of Budweiser. Give me water instead.

So I drink my red wines at *cellar* temperature. Over the course of the evening the temperature may rise to as much as seventy-five degrees but the wine is still fruity and shows no more heat, or alcohol, than it did in the cellar of the winery before it was bottled.

If you're buying a wine at the store and the wine is a little warm, you will be amazed what fifteen minutes in the refrigerator will do; suddenly the wine shows fruit, crispness and tastes like a real beverage.

With white wines, the temperature should not be so very different. I prefer fifty-five to sixty-five degrees; any colder and the wine has trouble showing its aromas and flavors. Remember that "well-chilled" line? In the case of the cheap stuff, you don't want to taste or smell it; the expensive stuff is all about taste and smell.

Most stores (and restaurants) sell their white wine too cold and their red wines too warm. I drive waiters crazy when I ask them to chill my red wine and leave my white wine sitting on the table out of the bucket. But then, torturing snooty waiters can be part of the fun.

What's the best way to uncork a bottle of wine?

"With your teeth", I want to reply. There are any number of contraptions for opening wine bottles and this has been so since the wine bottle became popular a little over two hundred years ago. In fact, a group exists for the purpose of celebrating the collections of wine openers, though I understand that few of the members of the organization actually drink wine.

Let that serve as our cautionary tale. It is easy to get caught up in the paraphenalia of wine, the openers, the nitrogen bottle-preservation systems, the three thousand dollars caves, and lose sight (or taste) of the real purpose, the drink.

Whatever method of uncorking suits you ought to be good enough, though smashing the neck of the bottle against the table is likely to worry your guests.

More civil are the popular openers, such as the simple waiter's corkscrew, a folding corkscrew with a knife, screw augur and hinged bottle grip. The waiter's corkscrew is very compact and very efficient. With this corkscrew, like all others, the idea is to cut the capsule (if it has a knife—some of the new California bottlings eschew them) below the lip of the bottle neck. Then one inserts the augur into the cork, firmly but gently twisting it into the cork until it catches and the augur can be screwed into the cork up to its final turn.

When levering this corkscrew upward, the real trick is to push against the bottle grip (as in the illustration) so that the cork always comes straight up and is not asked to bend in the middle where it might break. That simply means that the thumb holds the bottle press against the bottle lip so the hinge is allowed to do its job.

Once the cork is almost out of the bottle, simply grab the cork and gently twist it from the bottle. As a professional sommelier, I prefer that people not pop the cork at this point. Many bottles develop a slight vacuum during their sojourn in the cellar and if you pop the cork out, a small shot of wine may follow it.

The most popular corkscrew is the large winged thing best used for a garden spade. The augur is fat and seems anthropomorphically obsessed with the destruction of wine corks. The contraption is popular because it's the only one found at the Sears kitchen department and it has a reputation for ease that is belied by its true nature.

Best to save your shekels for the excellent Screwpull, a teflon-coated continuous screw. The only challenge this corkscrew presents is disbelief that anything could be so easy. Your merely press the corkscrew on top of the bottle, press down and begin screwing. As the augur is continuous, you keep screwing the corkscrew until the cork is completely removed. It is virtually idiot-proof.

Of course there are many other corkscrews you can try your hand at; the Ah-so, or twin-pronged opener that often results in corks floating inside bottles. One of my favorite silly openers involves an airpump that pushes the cork out by pumping air into the bottle through a needle. Try Screwpull instead.

Another recent device acts as a cork jack that allows one to lift the cork out in millimetric fractions. Try Screwpull instead.

The Europeans are happy, it seems, with the old augur on a stick routine; you know, where the person opening the bottle sticks it between their knees and yanks. Don't try this with white trousers.

IN THE STORE:

What's the best wine?

I really hate this question. I try to be understanding, I really do. The best wine? The best painting? The finest symphony? Your favorite child? Whadda question!

I'd sooner take a stab at the best sex I ever participated in. And, as in that example, I'd rather look forward to future experiences rather than dwell on the past.

Usually this question is followed by...

Yeh, but what's your favorite wine?

I don't, repeat, I don't have a favorite wine. I drink all kinds of wine. I drink white wines, red wines, sparkling wines, wines from Australia, Austria, Germany, Oregon, Chile, Italy, Missouri, hell, I even drink rosés. What I drink is often determined by the season; in summer I want crisp, tart German wines, rich Spanish whites, Loire and New Zealand wines, anything white, lean and mean. I think I drink a lot more white wine than red wine generally, but then that's blasphemous to most of my friends.

In the fall, I want reds, Rhones and Burgundies. In the winter, I love Bordeaux but nothing touches the sheer richness of the best reds of California and Australia, except maybe Italy's greatest. In the spring I drink with the weather; cold and rainy, I want red; warm and sunny, I want white.

My favorite wine? Anything good from anywhere, from any grape, drunk at the right time with the right friends. Hope that doesn't make me too picky.

What's the best advice you can give someone wanting to buy good wine?

No one should expect to be a wine expert. It's far too much work and costs too much for all the wines. Find and befriend a wine expert instead. The best place to start is a first-rate retailer, the sort of retailer that doesn't simply trot out Wine Spectator scores. A real retailer seeks out their own stars, find wineries and bottlings that may have escaped the attention of the big critics or that may have been underscored.

It may be the owner of the shop, it may be a knowledgeable clerk. Talk to someone who tastes frequently, who is as eager to show you a nine dollar bottle as the typical $25, 95-point monster. Tell the retailer what you like and let him or her show you new wines of the same region or grape. Ask for options from other countries and don't waste time asking for scores on each wine. Many of the most interesting wines don't have scores. Asking for the score is like saying you don't trust the retailer.

If you want your retailers to show imagination (and you do), don't negate their ideas by asking for a second opinion. Buy a bottle and taste it instead, then let your retailer know your reaction. A good retailer is willing to work with you and is always willing to hear your comments, however negative. The good retailer is honestly interested in finding what you like.

Shopping in a restaurant is not so very different, though I admit that your prospects of finding someone knowledgeable who cares are often bleak. Still, if you ask questions and parade a little ignorance, you might just get some good advice.

How do you buy the best?

That is a very dicey question. Though I think that many great wines are somewhat rough and rude in their youth, I cannot help but think of the great Bob Johnson cartoon—a customer spits out a wine calling it "disgusting". The jaded clerk notes that the wine received a "96" from the critics. "I'll take a case", the customer replies.

Use your own palate when assessing a wine. However, I'm afraid that I must side with hapless, naive customer in some cases. If the wine is sound and seems great, and if any of the trustworthy critics consider the wine to be of the greatest quality, buy it and age it.

If you don't like the wine, invest in something else. Obviously that means I expect you to taste the wines you buy. Oh, what a cruel taskmaster I am.

And one other question is begged...

Who are the critics I should trust?

This too is a personal decision, a matter of what you prefer. However, I believe that most of the well-known critics are capable of recognizing great wines, even though they may differ as to which wines are great.

I will admit to my own preferences amongst critics and can confidently recommend some such as Robert Parker. Parker deserves great respect, he is clearly in his element with wines of Bordeaux or the Rhone, as well as Alsace. When he reviews American wines, he is very trust-worthy, though he is eager to condemn California's produce and his condemnations should be taken with a grain of tartrate.

His reviews of German and Italian wines are less-informed. His writings upon Burgundy confuse me, is he seeking the same Burgundy I have always loved? He goes ga-ga over deeply-colored, oaky-rich, tannic red Burgundies and I think, has someone slipped a Rhone review in my Burgundy issue?

Even more famous is the *Wine Spectator*. It should be viewed as a Cosmo meets People Photoplay of the wine and food world. Some of the profiles are good, and some of the columnists are first-class. The reviews, well, they are, at best, inconsistent. Most of them should be ignored. Again, if they go ballistic over a particular wine, however, it's well worth a good look.

The Underground Wine Journal is a good compendium with excellent reviews of German wines and strong, intelligent views on Burgundy. *The Fine Wine Review* shares the same strengths.

The California Grapevine used to be important to me. I think that they are fairly consistent and quite fair, but I find that I differ more and more with them as time goes by.

Conniosseur's Guide has never been my cup of Latour. I almost never agree with them, but enjoy the most-praised wines (those that receive two or three puffs), especially for early consumption.

Stephen Tanzer's *International Wine Cellar* is reliable and reasoned and I find that, while I trust other writers more with certain regions of expertise, I consider this magazine very consistent across the map. Recommended.

Ronn Weigand's *Restaurant Wine* is an extremely consistent and intelligent list of reviews. I can easily recommend it. Even more valuable is Clive Coates' *The Vine*, which is flawless with French wine, and not uninformed with American, Italian, Spanish and German wines. Highly recommended.

How much should I spend to buy good wine?

You should spend more on wine than you're used to in order to get excellent wine. Excellent wine costs money so buy excellence when you want to put wines in the basement for aging.

However if you like to drink wine (I can think of no better use for a bottle) feel free to drink cheap, good wines as well as expensive, excellent ones. Lots of people only drink cheap, some people only drink expensive; I think they're all missing an opportunity.

A great bottle is like a great vacation, albeit cheaper and short-er-lived; it's something you ought to do at least once. There are moments that can be grown into events by the inclusion of a great bottle. When that time comes, buy something great, pay a fair price for it and enjoy the hell out of it.

The rest of the time enjoy wines from any price category. I am constantly amused by winelovers that seem unwilling to drink good wines, simply because they are straightforward, honest wines without the hoopla that accompanies great wines.

I like great wines, I really do, I suppose that if I won the lottery I might convince myself that I should only drink 100-point wines. Life however might get a bit boring if only because no critic ever awards 100 points to anything but blockbuster reds and sweet whites.

Call it my populist leanings but I think good wine's only necessary attribute is that it tastes good. I don't need every bottle to be a religious event, sometimes I just want a glass of wine.

So the secret is to enjoy all kinds of wine, as you want and when you want. But don't cut yourself off from any type of wine. Find a good drink for $6 and then drop $60 for a great one, at least for the passing of the millenium.

Do wine glasses make a difference?

For many American Italian bistros, the wine glass of choice is a juice glass. This tired cliche is extinct at fine restaurants in Italy, where some of the finest glassware I have ever seen is taken for granted.

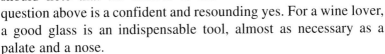

It's not a useless affectation. People who wish to take their wines a little more seriously should note that the answer to the question above is a confident and resounding yes. For a wine lover, a good glass is an indispensable tool, almost as necessary as a palate and a nose.

What is a good glass? It should be clear and mostly unfaceted so you can see the wine clearly. It should thin-rimmed and thin-walled and should be of a shape that delivers the prettiest possible aromas to your nose. After that opinions differ.

The famous glassmaking firm of Riedel has produced over sixty shapes and sizes for drinks from Riesling to single-malt scotch. All of these glasses are cleverly designed to accentuate the most enjoyable characteristics of each varietal, whether the focused-fruit-shape of the Chianti/Zinfandel glass or the extravagant bowl of the Burgundy glass.

Interestingly, each glass seems to deliver the right flavors in the mouth. By directing the wine to certain parts of the mouth certain flavors seem to be emphasized. I spend most of my time smelling my wines and I must admit that some of the Riedel glasses are better at focusing the flavors dramatically than on delivering the nose of a wine. Some of the Riedel glasses are less impressive than I might have hoped in delivering the best possible aromas.

Other companies offer excellent glassware. Schott Zwiesel has some excellent shapes in its line, though some of them are more decorative than ideal.

Other glassware lines, such as Les Impitoyables, Spiegelau and L'Oenologue from Cristal d'Arques, are first-rate. I often use INAO glasses, which are cheap and adequate to most of my large tasting settings.

Any good wine shop can direct you where to buy these glasses. Try buying a few and letting the addiction grow at a pace your wallet can handle.

Still, many writers and enthusiasts have left their heads behind in all their excitement. As Rubicon sommelier Larry Stone has queried, did no one enjoy wine in the dark ages before we discovered these new glasses?

Candidly, I simply want my glass to deliver my wine to me. In any glass, I look for a good focus to the bowl, usually prefering narrow and focused to wide and gross. This makes the glass as good as need be for most folks and most budgets.

AT YOUR AVERAGE CHIC BISTRO...

In a restaurant setting, you are at the mercy of your server, unless a wine steward is available. The server may be somewhat knowledgeable, or they may enthuse over a particular wine because it's the first wine they've ever tasted. As always, mentioning one of your favorites and seeing if anyone can think of something similar is a good policy.

The day of the wine steward, with clanking wine cup and snooty attitude, has nearly passed. Instead the few wine stewards left in America are often good, honest winelovers who genuinely want you to drink something you like. In my restaurants, we have a policy of 100% guarantee on any wine and I find more and more restaurants adopting the same posture.

In short, if a customer isn't drinking something they like, they're probably not going to enjoy their experience and will be less likely to return. So if a customer tastes a bottle and it's not what they had in mind, I make it disappear and bring something different.

From a business standpoint, I can always sell it by the glass. And I almost always end up making a good friend for the restaurant.

What are the rules for food and wine matching?

There are no rules. The old rules of white wines with white meat and red wine with red meat are in the dumpster where they belong. The new rules are not rules, they are recommendations.

However, don't assume that things are ever going to be as simple as the previous misguided concept. Consider instead that the new recommendations are going to be based upon the following happy coincidences:

Shellfish tends to go well with light-bodied, tart white wines. But some simple preparations of shellfish are perfect foils for the best Chardonnays.

Seafood dishes do well with dishes of similar weight. Steakier fish (such as tuna, salmon, halibut, et.al.) like heavier white wines. If the fish is grilled, a fruity red wine is best, though your bottle of tasty, toasty Chardonnay can work too.

Chicken and other fowl handle wines of similar weight, that is, if the chicken is skinless and poached, a fairly light white wine is great. If the chicken has its skin on with other intensely flavored notes (such as garlic, wine reduction, etc) medium-bodied, white wines or fruity red wines are excellent.

Tannin is the component in red wine that gives a dusty, even bitter sensation. Tannin's roughness is softened by fat, so the amount of fat in a particular dish helps determine which wine will handle the dish best. Fat can come from many sources; certainly beef is famously rich in fat, but so is lamb when it's served on the bone and not cut from the loin. Cheese and cheese sauces are high in milk fat, while mushrooms add a distinctive fat-rich flavor, though there is no fat in the fungi.

Pork is low in fat and so lighter red wines and even many white wines are delightful with many pork dishes.

Game can be lean or high in fat; combine with bigger, more tannic wines if the cut is on the bone. Beef is invariably in need of big, intense reds fashioned from Merlot, Cabernet Sauvignon, Syrah, Nebbiolo or Brunello.

Dessert and wine are quite tricky, but the best rule is to be certain that the wine is always sweeter than the dessert.

More important than any of these ideas is that you drink what you like when you like it. Because it really is more important, I'll say it again, drink what you like when you like it.

Why do people smell the cork?

Because they've been trained to by a handful of snooty wine stewards who haven't the faintest idea themselves why anyone does it. Something about checking the wine to see if it's bad, though few of them could spot a bad wine in a fifty dollar Riedel glass. Nevertheless they persevere, shoving corks into the visages of countless, hapless minions.

Make them stop. A cork's purpose is to hold the wine in the bottle until you want to drink it. If something is wrong with the wine, smell and taste the wine; it's the most likely indicator.

Smelling the cork to see if the wine is bad is like turning on the TV to see if you have a flat tire. No, it's more like turning on the weather channel to see if it's hailing outside.

The next time a waiter hands you a cork, ignore its very existence and check the wine. If the server waits for you to check the cork before proceeding, tap your empty glass with your finger while giving him or her your best "New here, are we?" look. That server deserves it.

But what do I do if a wine is bad?

If this happens, hopefully you are confident enough with your opinion not to get emotional about it. You check it a second time, re-taste it and then tell the server.

What you're looking for:

1) a bad, over-the-hill or heat-damaged wine. If you don't like the wine, you've simply made a bad selection. It's a personal thing,

if you get my drift. Deal with it. An over-the-hill red wine exhibits little color or aroma. A tired white wine is distinctly golden in color (although sweet wines are golden and even brownish in color before they go bad). What flavor is there, is all about tart, bizarre acidity and is decidedly bland or even unpleasant. Check the vintage and if it's a recent bottling, something is decidedly wrong.

If the wine has a cooked or stewed tomato aroma, and especially if there is extreme stickiness around the mouth and neck of the bottle or if there are dried rivulets on the side of the bottle, the wine is probably heat-damaged. Reject it and choose another wine; all of the bottles the establishment owns are probably from the same, badly-stored case.

2) A "corked" wine (see page 11). At least 5% are tainted by a chemical we call TCA, or tricloroanisole, ruining the wines with a stinky, dank "corky" aroma. No amount of "breathing" will save the wine.

Cork's vulnerability to this malady is bad enough. But natural cork is not a permanent closure. Cork is too weak for use beyond twenty-five years or so, especially if the wine has been moved several times.

Some Bordeaux estates make some publicity out of a re-corking procedure. In this, the old cork is removed, the wine topped up with a fresher (!) vintage and then recorked. As costly as this is, I think that the best option is simply to move wine as little as possible and to remember that the older the wine, the more fragile the cork.

The new synthetic corks seem to have unending life, can even be reused and never exihibit TCA. I expect that synthetic cork will grow radically in popularity in the next five years.

Is it good to breathe wines?

The whole concept of wine breathing leaves me gasping for air. At the very least the idea of heavy breathing is greatly overrated. The concept of breathing is based upon oxygen's effect upon a newly-opened bottle of wine—it produces aroma and flavor compounds. Oxygen can also lessen tannin's dusty, slightly bitter sensation. The problem is that the fruit can disappear before the tannins soften.

An example: in my waiter days a friend brought in a bottle of 1934 Volnay to enjoy with his dinner at our restaurant. He offered a taste and, as it was curiously devoid of taste, I asked him when he opened it. "I've been letting it breathe for two hours", was the naive reply.

My other complaint with the heavy-breathing school is that some young, tough wines, the sort of wines that supposedly gain from breathing, often show their plumpest fruit when the bottle is freshly opened. A hour or so of breathing means that you may drink a wine more perceptively tannic than that you would have tasted when it was first opened.

Lastly (forgive my diatribe) a bottle of wine is a very skinny place to get oxygen to a wine. Truthfully, the best place for a wine to breathe is in the glass or, even better, in your mouth.

What are legs in a glass of wine?

As one swirls the wine in a good glass, many wines will cling to the side of the glass, leaving behind tears that ease slowly down the glass. These tears are often called legs but, in the words of the great Michael Broadbent, "I'm not much of a leg man."

Legs, or strong, even-colored tears, are an indication of high glycerol content, itself a byproduct of high alcohol. To say that a wine has great legs is to remark that it has high alcohol, not a note of desirability unless you're looking for quick oblivion.

The reputation of legs as arbiters of quality probably stems from France's traditional difficulty in fully-ripening grapes. Hence a wine with high alcohol probably came from a very ripe year, most usually a great year.

MATTERS OF THE ART

Are French wines the best?

Thirty years ago the answer was yes, but best is a malleable concept. One hundred years ago, top German vineyards such as Wehlener Sonnenuhr received two and three times the amount that bidders were willing to pay for Chateau Lafite or Chateau Latour.

Today, the wine world is a drastically changed place. Great wines are made from every good wine-producing country; in Australia, Austria, Lebanon and South Africa.

For those who learned to drink wine by pursuing the great, super-rich and powerful wines of California, that rich fruit, tannin and warmth happens only in California. For those weaned on the great growths of France, America's and Australia's wines seem coarse, awkward and vulgar.

So to say that the wines of one country are best is to make the classic error that wine lives in a rational, objective world where a tasting scientist can ascertain the score of a wine with a tolerance factor of less than .1%. What a crock.

We all have different measuring sticks when it comes to greatness, as it should be.

Where I can seem to be a Francophile is in my appreciation of the breadth of great French wines. From sweet white wines (Sauternes, Selection de Grains Nobles in Alsace) to dry white wines (the great Sauvignons of Sancerre and Pouilly Fume and of white Graves, the greatest Chardonnays in the world in Burgundy, Pinot Gris and Riesling from Alsace to name only a handful), in sparkling wine (Champagne is the pinnacle, have no doubt), with soft reds and dry roses, with fruity reds (Pinot Noir is unparalleled in Burgundy), with spicy reds (I could drink myself to death in the Rhone and I'd still have money left) and great ageworthy reds (Bordeaux and other areas), France is unmatched.

France is not the "best" but most of the world's classic wines were first defined here and France remains the champion in sheer numbers of great wines.

Still, it reminds me of a comment of a South American friend of mine many years ago. He told me that he loved Kansas City because there were so many beautiful women here. I differed, saying the most beautiful women lived in Rome.

"There is no such thing as 'more' or 'most' beautiful women," he schooled me. "They are simply beautiful." No argument, if you will forgive our sexism. Beautiful is simply beautiful, dude, and dudette and great wine needn't be more than great.

Does America make wines as great as Europe?

I think I've already answered this question but I include it here because it usually follows my previous response. I usually look closely at the questioner and wonder if he just took the bag off his head.

As noted above, Europe makes styles of wine, from Port to Sherry to Champagne that America simply cannot compete with at this time. Still America too has styles of wine that are not necessarily emulated or growable in Europe. Our biggest reds are tannic, forward, fruity monsters and you'd have to be a real dweeb not to catch the vulgar charm.

America's present and future glory in wine lies in finding out that which America does best. Europe has had nearly two thousand years to sort that out, America has had less than one hundred.

We are only now assessing the vineyards and the varietals to see what combinations are best. California is in the midst of the largest (and best-financed) replantation the wine world has seen since the phylloxera (see below) devastation of the late 19th Century.

California's vineyards have been pillaged by this microscopic bug, so many vineyards are being torn up and replanted with resistant materials. This replantation allows Californians to rethink the matching of sites and grapes.

The hope is that we can make better choices in having the right area for Merlot or Chardonnay, et.al. The system in place up till now, was random at best and reflected the fact that for most of our history our farmers have planted certain grapes, not because the site was ideal, but because that grape was popular.

Nevertheless in the last ten years we have made wines every bit as good as Europe's finest. Imagine what better selection will do for us.

As noted above, great wine is great. Those people who ask me for greater clarification in these things simply want to be sure that I include America in this great assessment, and I do.

What is phylloxera?

This microscopic louse nearly destroyed the world's oldest and most important agricultural industry. The phylloxera bug lives in the ground and chews upon the roots of vines, eventually killing them. A strong infestation can destroy an entire vineyard in one season.

Phylloxera is an American bug. When Europeans arrived here, they found grapevines everywhere (Vineland it was called) but were unhappy with the stinky aromas from these American vine-grapes. When they tried to plant their own European varietals (of a different species called vitis vinifera) the phylloxera bug took to the new vines like cotton candy. Even ardent lovers, such as Thomas Jefferson, eventually concluded that vinifera viticulture was impossible here.

In the mid-nineteenth century, some growers began grafting European vines onto American roots with remarkable results. The plants were, it seemed, impervious to phylloxera, which coexists with American vines by feeding on but not destroying them.

Around 1856, phylloxera was discovered in France, near the southern Rhone Valley. By 1881, the bug was in Germany and by 1900 the entire European continent was decimated. To this day, a third of France's vineyards of that time have never been replanted to vineyards.

Though nationalistic sentiment fought against it, eventually the vineyards were replanted using American rootstock, with the best European vines still grafted on top, vines of Chardonnay, Pinot Noir, Cabernet Sauvignon and the rest. Though it took two or three decades to replant the millions of acres, since that time Europe's vineyards have been safe from the pest.

Today, California is having to replant almost 90% of her vineyards because of new phylloxera devastation, the result of a proposed new type of phylloxera. Though Californians maintain otherwise, the ugly truth is, that the bug is succeeding in California now, because growers there became greedy and planted onto rootstocks only half-American, which gave them higher yields.

Now, at a cost of hundreds of millions, California's growers are replanting using 100% American rootstocks, the same rootstocks the Europeans reluctantly used one hundred years ago to save their own ravaged vineyards.

Why is Merlot softer than Cabernet Sauvignon?

Merlot is a very, very popular wine right now and sometimes that mystifies me. Why have Americans chosen this grape above other perhaps more noble grapes? Our discovery of the long-established benefits of red wine consumption has hastened a return to red wines and Merlot is considered a soft, red wine, one that can appeal to a divergent nation of drinkers.

Personally, I figure that Merlot is easy to say and that probably helped.

The softness factor is slightly more problematic. Merlot has a thinner skin than its usual partners Cabernet Sauvignon and Cabernet Franc and as a result is lower in tannins. Thus it is often regarded in the Medoc region of Bordeaux as a grape providing a softening effect on Cabernet. The inference is that Merlot ages more quickly and is always a soft, fruity wine.

Unfortunately for this scenario, the right bank of Bordeaux is predominately Merlot and some of these wines can take a long time to age and soften. Chateau Petrus, with 100% Merlot, is the most famous example. This remarkable wine is nearly undrinkable from five years old until its early maturity, which can happen at ten years of age or thirty.

Petrus is part of the problem with American Merlot. Famously, Petrus grows its Merlot vines on a clay cap of soil above broken gravel. American growers heard about the clay and forgot the gravel and, as a result, have planted Merlot in wet, clay-heavy sites in California.

In those conditions Merlot tastes weedy, light, soft and ages quickly, living only five or so years. The result? California Merlot is a varied thing, with great rich Merlot overwhelmed in number by boring, herbaceous juice.

Though Merlot is lower in tannin than Cabernet Sauvignon that is no excuse for some of the light, insipid wines that masquerade as Merlot in California. Where Merlot is concerned here in America, a few extra dollars can often buy you a great deal more wine.

Are wines like Y'quem really worth that much money?

Chateau Y'quem is certainly one of the world's most expensive wines, opening at a price of near $200 per bottle and going up from there. This dessert blend of Semillon (usually 80 percent) and Sauvignon Blanc (20 percent) is picked one cluster, sometimes one berry, at a time in order to attain the greatest level of richness. Y'quem has several rivals, with estates like Chateau Coutet offering reserve bottlings (called Cuvee Madame) surely as great as Y'quem.

Still what makes Y'quem worth the extra hundred or so dollars is a consistency and character that makes buying Yquem in a great vintage an absolutely ironclad guarantee of greatness in your cellar. And that makes a wine very valuable.

It's amazing to think that wine is such a variable thing that an estate, which is completely reliable, could command outrageous prices.

But, in candor, Y'quem is so wickedly rich and brilliantly balanced that were it the world's most inconsistent value, it would still cost a car payment and be worth every penny!

Are sweet wines only for beginners?

The answer is no, but usually they're for dessert. So-called sweet wines require further definition. The super-rich dessert wines of the world; aged Sauternes and Barsac, Selection de Grains Nobles, Muscat Beaumes de Venise, Banyuls and others from France, Recioto and Liquoroso from Italy, Moscato de Setubal, Port and Madeira from Portugal, sweet Oloroso from Sherry in Spain, the Beerenauslesen, Trockenbeerenauslesen and Eiswein of Germany, and the great "stickies" of Australia, America and South Africa, are intended to bring to a close, a great meal, though they can sometimes be enjoyed on their own.

A number of these wines can in fact be enjoyed at other times of the meal; the most famous example being Sauternes' (especially young Sauterne) great affinity for foie gras. Moscato d'Asti (the better version of Asti Spumanti) is a pretty awesome mid-day or evening snack with antipasti.

Often when people ask me about sweet wines, they're really asking about the crappy beverage wines of our youth, the ones with names like Annie Green Springs and Kountry Kwencher. Strange surnames and misspellings aside, most of us did start with these alcoholic imitations of Koolaid and, having become the sophisticated bon vivants we are today, eschew such bathwater.

So Gallo simply carbonated and repackaged them as Bartles & Jaymes, but that's another story.

We sophisticates, however, tossed the baby out with this bathwater. In the eyes of most winedrinkers, dry is good, sweet is bad. The truth is, it depends. Sweet wines, grown in a warm climate, and which have no balancing acidity are pretty bad. Sweet wines, and somewhat sweet wines, grown in a cool climate, with great tart acidity in the finish, are one of my greatest pleasures. The great hillsides estates of Germany; Wehlener Sonnenuhr, Brauneberger Juffer Sonnenuhr, Oberemmeler Huette, Eitelsbacher Karthaueser-shofberg, and other unpronounceable places, offer wines with such bracing acidity and lemony character in the finish, that the only way in which they could be tasty is if they had some sweetness to balance the tartness.

The wines are labeled to give a rough approximation of their sweetness levels, with sweetness increasing as the labels change from Kabinett to Spaetlese to Auslese and beyond to the desserts (Beerenauslese, Trockenbeerenauslese and Eiswein).

Each region produces wines in these categories, but styles vary with the region. The Mosel-Saar-Ruwer rivers are home to wines of great delicacy and finesse. The Rheingau, Rheinhessen and Rheinpfalz tend to give bigger, fleshier wines, though the Rheingau is often regarded as the top district.

Germany has for centuries produced wines of unparalleled richness, fruitiness and balance. Despite this Germany has suffered in the late twentieth century but many of her ills are self-imposed.

Germany has for years concentrated upon delivering cheap, low acid, sweet wines like Piesporter Michelsberg (not the great Goldtroepfchen vineyard), Zeller Schwarz Katz, Liebfraumilch or Moselbluemchen at $4.99 and under in stores. Not surprisingly, these wines have little or no character and about as much of an attempt has been made to explain to consumers the difference between Germany's crap and her stars.

The result is that all of Germany's wines are seen as soda pop-ish wines for those who are just starting. Even people who should know better won't drink them because their prejudice runs so deep.

For me, it's back to the beginners. My eyes light up when a customer admits that they don't know much about wine and that they really like sweet wines. I drag out my favorite von Hoevel or JJ Pruem or Zilliken or Kuenstler or Gunderloch or any of Germany's

N

• Hamburg

Elbe

Berlin •

Hannover •

Rhein

Elbe

Sachsen

• Dresden

Saale-Unstrut

Saale

Bonn •

Ahr

Mittelrhein

Mosel-Saar-Ruwer

Rheingau

Nahe

Hessische-Bergstrasse

• Frankfurt

Franken

• Trier

Rheinhessen

Pfalz

Wurttemberg

Baden

Rhein

Neckar

GERMANY

other great producers. When they taste it, they're happy because it tastes good to them; me, I'm trying to change the world, one customer at a time.

What's the difference between Fume Blanc and Sauvignon Blanc?

History and Robert Mondavi created this one. When vinifera grapes were first grown in Europe, they were spread around as traders and the wind saw fit. Over the centuries grapes such as the Sauvignon Blanc found homes in several areas; most notably in Bordeaux (as Sauvignon Blanc, Punechon or Surin), in the eastern Loire (as Blanc Fume or Gentin a Romorantin) and northern Italy, as plain Sauvignon.

Fast forward to the early 60's, as Robert Mondavi has left his family's business at Charles Krug, to start his own eponymous winery. Sauvignon Blanc was widely produced then, most of it clean and boring and slightly sweet. Mondavi had returned in 1962 from a tour to France wildly enthusiastic about oak barrels and wine. He decided to experiment with French barrels and was pleased with the results with Chardonnay, Cabernet Sauvignon, Pinot Noir, even Sauvignon Blanc. The style he had in mind was such a radical departure for Californian Sauvignon that he decided he needed a new name.

By flipping the Loire name blanc fume around, he coined a term that has found great favor in America, Fume Blanc. Originally, the term might have suggested a Sauvignon Blanc that has been aged in oak, but that correlation has long ago ceased. Mondavi characteristically did not protect the name but offered it for general use so today's Fume Blancs could be squeeky-clean stainless steel-fermented, light drinkers or they could be so smothered in oak as to taste like Chardonnay. This is a good example of why you need to know a good retailer.

Is Champagne different from other sparkling wines?

First of all, Champagne is a place, it's an hour or so outside of

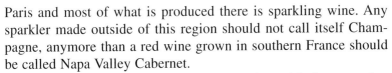

Paris and most of what is produced there is sparkling wine. Any sparkler made outside of this region should not call itself Champagne, anymore than a red wine grown in southern France should be called Napa Valley Cabernet.

In all the quality wine-producing countries, with the exception of the U.S. and Australia, the use of the word "Champagne" is illegal when applied to wines not from Champagne. In America, sparklers from Andre to Korbel still use the term though no producer of quality is interested in usurping Champagne's name.

Champagne is an amazing area of warm hills in the center of cold, northern France, and beneath the vineyards is well-drained soil rich in chalk, sometimes at depths of thiry feet or more.

This chalk brings a delicacy and intensity to sparkling wines that is unmatched by any other area. The greatest Champagnes have qualities that no other region will ever achieve.

On the other hand, Champagne is completely planted—there are no more unplanted hillsides and so the top producers have begun vineyard projects in other countries and now branches of Taittinger, Moet et Chandon, Roederer, Mumm and others can be found in California, South Africa, Chile, Australia and Tasmania.

Some of these new wineries, and others not owned by the great Champagne houses, are producing first-rate bubbly. In California, Roederer Estate, Iron Horse and Scharffenberger make great and lovely bottles of sparkling wine, while Maison Deutz, Jordan, S. Anderson, Domaine Chandon and others are quite reliable.

That these bottles are not top Champagne's equivalent is of little importance. They are excellent and affordable and work for every occasion.

In our conversations about Champagne it is implied that the best are rich and dry. The cheap ones are probably sweet.

Most Champagne is slightly sweet but the presence of bubbles makes it taste drier than it really is. That is to say, if there weren't some sweetness to the wine, the bubbles would make it taste too dry and even bitter. So a sweet bubbly is not a crazy or plebian idea.

As a dessert wine Asti Spumanti is pretty wonderful. As a table wine, it's lightness and sweetness make it a poor companion for most foods (it ends up tasting like sugar water) but if it's your drink, more power to you.

I prefer the rarer Moscato d'Asti, from the best vineyards around Asti and selected from the less-interesting Asti Spumanti. Moscato d'Asti is avidly consumed by the citizens of the Piedmont and even many producers of Piedmont's monster Baroli and Barbareschi save a piece of their vineyards for Moscato production.

It is generally lighter in sweetness, alcohol and fewer in bubbles than Asti Spumanti, but with Asti's great freshness, flowers and fruitiness. It's a great patio drink.

Are there any good wines grown in Missouri (substitute Kansas, Virginia, Arkansas, Montana or any of the fledging state wine industries)?

Five years ago, the question, as applied to most of the US, would have been ludicrous. Today there are an amazing number of good quality wines from almost every state in the Union. Naturally, the West Coast states of California, Washington and Oregon are the finest representatives for American wine, but New York offers excellence as well from the Finger Lakes and parts of Long Island.

Texas, Virginia, Maryland, Idaho, Arizona, New Mexico, Connecticutt and Pennsylvania all have very good estates producing fine wine. Most of these are produced from vinifera, or European, vines. These are the vines with such familiar names as Chardonnay, Merlot and Cabernet Sauvignon.

The other interesting developments in American wine involve hybrid vines.

What exactly is a hybrid vine?

Thanks for that question. A brief chunk of history: when the phylloxera bug destroyed Europe's vines, American rootstock (as outlined above) came to the rescue. It was natural that some European producers should experiment with the American vines to see if good wine could be produced from them

A number of hybrids, or crossings between European and American vines, were developed by Professor Seibel in France and Dr. Mueller in Germany in the early years of the 20th Century. Most of these saw little favor but some hybrids, such as Baco Noir, still thrive in the world's vineyards. The island of Madeira is currently struggling with an effort to replant vineyards filled with Baco Noir.

Hybrids are usually seen as, at best, vines which can be relied upon to produce tolerable but boring wine. In the last few years, however, enormous strides have been made with these grapes in U.S. States from Michigan to Missouri and especially in England. It is no longer fair to regard these wines as bad.

Instead, these vines are proving that they can be regarded as good to very good producers of wine, and this will allow other states and areas to improve upon their own regional wines.

To me, that is a very good development. I have seen firsthand that regional chauvinism can bring non-winedrinkers to try a regional wine and, if it is good, to take up wine drinking. I think it's kind of cute when Ma and Pa Kettle can have an argument about wine.

What are the Rhone Rangers?

The Rhone Valley in France offers some of the greatest values in red wine and so its wines have not escaped the palates of some of our more educated winemakers. As well, the climatic conditions of much of the southern Rhone and Provence are not dissimilar to much of warm, sunny California.

A group of these winemakers, informally called the Rhone Rangers, have spent a great part of their careers in the last decade exploring these varietals. Syrah, Mourvedre, Viognier, Roussanne, Marsanne and Grenache are showing up in Rhone-style blends and in pure bottlings from a number of wineries in California.

The most famous of them, the great and iconoclastic Randall Grahm of Bonny Doon Vineyards, has made quite a loud noise about the Rhone varietals' appropriateness to California's climate. Some years ago, I saw him declaim, on a panel of winemakers, his view that Chardonnay and Cabernet Sauvignon are completely inappropriate to California.

His diatribe was in response to a question posed, "What is the greatest myth in winemaking today?" After blasting Chardonnay for five minutes, Randall sat down and his friend Tom Peterson, of Chateau Souverain, was asked the same question. "Randall Grahm", he replied!

Today, I'd still rather drink Bonny Doon.

THE GEOGRAPHY OF WINE

There is a lot of minutiae that wine geeks like me love to prattle on about. Some of it is pointless and some of it strikes to the heart of what I love about wine.

Of these, nothing is more enjoyable than the evidence that a great wine is of a particular place. Good wines can be fashioned from many devices; from blends of differing, even divergent regions, from blends of complimentary grapes, from blends of differing styles of methods of vinification. Great wines, to me, always reflect a particular soil, a spot of land, a hill and the old, well-tended vines on it.

Why are some vineyard areas better than others?

As divergent as the world's wines are, and as divergent as are the regions from which they derive, there is an enjoyable commonality to the greatest vineyards.

All of these vineyards are filled with old vines, sited in well-drained and vine-healthy soils. These vineyards are almost always situated near a river and are on hills, whether vertiginous or gently sloping towards the sun.

Most importantly, the world's great vineyards are somewhat slow in their ability to ripen grapes. That is to say, La Tache in Burgundy is a great vineyard, partly because it takes a long time to ripen the grapes.

Ripening grapes in the Central Valley of California is quite easy, but the wines have no balance and little flavor. The quality of a wine is greatly dependent upon the length of the growing season.

So the world's best vineyards are in areas where the growing season is long, and where the climate is cool enough for the grapes to require this long season in order to ripen.

Many of the Old World's finest vineyards struggle for ripeness in most years and in some, they never really achieve ripeness—this is why the vintage can carry such importance.

In the New World, the most exciting new regions are those that only a decade ago were seen as too cool for proper ripening. New World winemakers have realized that a long growing season is necessary for high quality and so areas such as Carneros and Western Sonoma in California and Margaret River and the Southern Vales in Australia are seen as areas of tremendous new opportunity.

The produce of these regions has already proven its worth; imagine what another century of experimentation will do.

What are the best regions in California?

Ten years ago, Napa was the undisputed leader in the minds of most Americans and public perception of Napa is still greatest. Many of the best new wineries are in other regions however.

The Carneros has seen a great deal of investment and is nearly completely planted. For me, this area will continue to offer strong Pinot Noir and Chardonnay but my interest in these varietals finds greater hope down south, towards Santa Barbara.

North of Santa Barbara, and as far as Edna Valley, there are new plantings of those two grapes, as well as Rhone varietals like Syrah and Viognier. I am completely convinced that much of California's best awaits us there.

Between Monterey and Santa Barbara are many newly-planted vineyards and many old ones. The Paso Robles region is the site for the Perrin brothers' (of Chateau de Beaucastel fame) American experiment with Rhone grapes. Preliminary reports are very good.

Paso Robles has many older vineyards, of Zinfandel and Caber-

N

Mendocino

Anderson
Valley

Lake

Sierra
Foothills

Russian
River

Alexander Valley

El Dorado

Napa Valley
Sonoma
Carneros

• **Sacramento**

Lodi

San Francisco •

Livermore Valley

Santa Cruz Mountains

Santa Clara Valley

Santa Lucia Highlands

Arroyo Seco

Monterey

Paso Robles

San Luis
Obispo

Edna Valley

Santa
Barbara

Santa Maria Valley

Santa Ynez Valley

Los Angeles •

Temecula

San Diego •

CALIFORNIA

net Sauvignon primarily. The hilly parts of Paso Robles are still available and a number of wineries are trying all manner of grapes, from Chardonnay to Viognier.

Moving north from Paso Robles, good but somewhat awkward wines have been made for many years in the Monterey area and the answer lies in finding the appropriate clones and varietals here. The old herbaceous Monterey character has been ameliorated and now the tannins need taming but Cabernet, Merlot, Sauvignon Blanc and Chardonnay all have a bright future.

From Monterey to San Francisco, great Chardonnays and Cabernets have appeared from here since the nineteenth century. If the grapegrowers can keep ahead of the developers, the Santa Cruz Mountains will continue to offer some of our most exciting new wines.

Napa and Sonoma are still acknowledged as our volume quality leaders and, amazingly, new labels seem to crop up weekly, all with 95-point scores and a few hundred cases to sell. This Balkanization of the Napa is not all bad, as it allows small enclaves to become known. And larger ones, such as Howell Mountain or Mount Veeder, are inhabited by more winemakers attempting to tame the fierce tannins of these two areas.

Someone's bound to get it right. Sonoma is likely to see this same splintering and we will learn more about each of the sub-regions of Sonoma in the process.

Most important has been the growth of wineries in western Sonoma, in pockets of cool, marine-influenced hills where the scientists claimed only a decade ago that viticulture was impossible. Cool-climate grapes, such as Pinot Noir and Chardonnay are very promising here.

These vineyards are as interesting as those in Mendocino (particularly Anderson Valley) in the north, where excellent wines, from Zinfandel to Sauvignon Blanc to great sparkling wine, are proof of the great potential here.

Further east, the Sierra Foothills are still a rough and dry region, not much changed from the Gold Rush days that spawned these

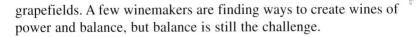

grapefields. A few winemakers are finding ways to create wines of power and balance, but balance is still the challenge.

Is Bordeaux the most important French wine?

Imagine trying to answer this one in seven sentences or less. I can't recall my response (I probably mumbled something about liking Chenin Blanc too), but it should have included a short essay in the amazing diversity of French viticulture. No Jacques Le Pen-like slimeball has been allowed to champion only one race of grape here; instead most of our greatest grapes strut their stuff throughout France's landscape.

It seems appropriate to start in Bordeaux, germanely, because most people believe that Bordeaux occupies a guaranteed throne in wine heaven. At its height, Bordeaux is defined by the remarkable majesty of Chateaux Latour, Lafite, Mouton, Haut Brion, Cheval Blanc, Petrus, Y'quem and many other names that have crept into the cultural mind.

Even at its nadir, Bordeaux can represent good, basic dry red wine, with a certain classiness that belies its ordinary birth. Part of that smartness has to be reflective of the varietal blending that defines Bordeaux. The best wines are blends of Cabernet Sauvignon, Cabernet Franc, Merlot, Malbec and Petite Verdot. On the right bank, Merlot or Cabernet Franc makes up the greatest proportion; on the left bank, or Medoc, Cabernet Sauvignon is the focus. The lesser wines of Bordeaux are composed most often of similar blends with Merlot as the primary constituent.

Most of the familiar Bordeaux chateaux are part of the classification of 1855, in which a group of businessmen stated the obvious; that certain estates, such as Lafite and Latour, received the highest prices for their wines. Others received lower prices and that most of these could be divided into six groups, categorized by price.

The top four (now five) were called the first-growths, the next fifteen were called the second-growths and so on to the last eighteen, known as the fifth-growths. All other wines were excluded from any classification and in 1924 became known as Cru Bour-

geois, suggesting a rank just below the aristocratic sixty-one classified growths.

These include Chateau Larose Trintaudon, the Medoc's largest
estate, as well as all other important estates outside the Medoc sub-
region. Thus the regions of Graves (with the exception of Haut
Brion) went unclassified, and too the regions of St. Emilion and
Pomerol.

Some of these regions have created classifications of their own
and because there is no uniformity to it all, the only classification
that holds in the public's mind is that of 1855.

Pomerol, the region offering Bordeaux's most expensive red
wines has no established heirarchy, but Petrus is understood to
exist on a plain unreached by any other. Still such estates as
Trotanoy, le Pin, la Fleur de Gay, Lafleur, la Conseillante and L'E-
vangile can be glorious and, sadly, almost as expensive.

Merlot predominates in St. Emilion as well as Pomerol, but
Cabernet Franc is sometimes just as important, especially with St.
Emilion's delicious flagship Cheval Blanc. Cabernet Sauvignon
shows itself only as a blending agent, except in the excellent
Chateau Figeac where it comprises the majority.

The other great estates of St. Emilion exhibit that lovely sup-
pleness that comes of Merlot, but show, perhaps, a sterner side than
most New World Merlot. The wines age very well at their best and,
with the slightest examples, they are still soft and fruity.

White wine in Bordeaux is highly-regarded but only recently
deserving of that status. Chateau Haut Brion and Domaine de
Chevalier, among a few others, have always made great wine and
this high quality has hidden the sins of many others.

In the last fifteen years, great improvements have been made,
mostly in the wineries. Nowadays, many producers in Graves (now
called Pessac-Leognan) are releasing excellent barrel-aged Sauvignon Blancs, rich and ripe and smoky.

The dessert wines of the region are amazing wines (see Chateau
Y'quem – page 42) of richness and crispness. Usually composed of
Semillon with lesser amounts of Sauvignon Blanc, they are very

full-bodied (sometimes as much as fourteen percent alcohol) with honey and creme brulee flavors balanced by their power and firm acidity.

The rest of the southwestern corner of France is populated by esoteric wines that, being unknown, can offer some value. Be sure to buy on someone's recommendation however; there is unevenness to the work here, but consider wines such as Madiran, Cahors, Cotes de Buzet (all reds), Bergerac, Monbazillac and Jurancon (all good whites).

From Bordeaux eastward, there is a vast ocean of vines, and throughout the 19th century and most of the twentieth, their wines were dreadful or boring. The last ten years strange things have happened here; great improvements in the vineyards have brought excellent values onto the American shelves, with names like Fortant de France, Jenard and Les Jamelles.

Areas previously lumped together as the Midi, as bland and as warm as the name conjures, have been rediscovered and are gaining deserved fame. If you like the red wines of the southern Rhone, you can do worse than to experiment with the delicious wines of Minervois, Coteaux de Languedoc, Fitou or Corbieres.

Sunny Provence is also part of the old Midi, but has long distinguished itself for both reds and whites. Cassis and Palette can give very good whites, while lovely reds are found throughout the Cotes (hills) de Provence where, for me, the pinnacle is Bandol.

The southern Rhone is not so very different from Provence, though it can often show a great breed benefiting its status as a great wine region with a millenia-long tradition. Though vineyards such as Gigondas and Vacqueyras and, occasionally, Sablet and Cairanne can try to offer a challenge, the southern Rhone is ruled by the great Chateauneuf-du-Pape. For me Chateauneuf is the best red wine bargain in France. Chateau de Beaucastel, Chapoutier, Vieux Telegraphe and Rayas make masterful wines here and deserve anything they can get for them.

The southern Rhone is comprised of blends of varietals, based greatly upon the Grenache grape, rich with flavors of strawberry

FRANCE

and black pepper. The northern Rhone reds are reliant solely upon the Syrah grape. This wonderful grape gives flavors of cassis, blackberry and lemon and always has a certain smokiness, like someone's roasting a leg of lamb next door.

The northern Rhone is very different from the south, still ruled by the sun and the hot dry wind called the Mistral but more continental in its temperature swings. A series of hills offer some of the finest vineyards in the world, with Cote Rotie, Cornas and Hermitage giving extraordinarily rich wines.

These wines can be quite pricey, but then the quantities involved are ten percent of that produced by most Bordeaux chateaux, and consumers seem far less resistant to those high prices.

The Rhone's whites are a mixed lot, with many neutral bottlings but a handful of great ones; such as most Chateauneuf and Hermitage Blancs and Condrieu.

To the north, closer to Paris, is Burgundy, home to the finest Chardonnay and Pinot Noir in the world. As great as these wines are, they are often very expensive though, like the northern Rhone, they are produced in such miniscule amounts, it is a wonder that they aren't even more expensive.

Burgundy can prove a vexatious pursuit, especially when it comes to the great tease, Pinot Noir. It is not uncommon to see good red Burgundy do an about-face and taste simply awful after ten years in the bottle. Only careful buying and monitoring of the wine's sojourn in time can prevent that unpleasant occurence.

But those of us who love Burgundy madly pursue it because, though the risk is there, the reward is to drink the loveliest, most elegant drink in the world. Low in tannin, red Burgundy shows great fruit at three years of age, and can be still seductive and brilliantly complex at twenty years.

White Burgundy is an altogether more austere drink than its American Chardonnay counterpart, but then White Burgundy can age for eight years or many more. California Chardonnay should rarely see more than five years in the bottle.

The well-known wines of Macon Village and Pouilly Fuisse hail from the southern part of Burgundy and show more of the tart pear fruit that typifies Chardonnay here. Most austere is Chardonnay's outpost in the cold hills south of Paris called Chablis. These are crisp and tart and seem to smell of wet rocks (in a pleasant way). I am very fond of ten-year-old Chablis and will follow a bottle anywhere.

To the west, the vineyards of the Loire Valley begin with Sauvignon Blanc's other great repose in France, the twin hills of Sancerre and Pouilly Fume. These wines can be herbaceous to the point of stinkiness but some of them; Fournier, Celestin-Blondeau, Dagenneau and Cailhbourdin included, are among the most complex crisp whites in the world.

The Loire Valley is home to a number of other grapes as well. Pinot Noir shows up on occasion; light and fruity as Sancerre Rouge. Gamay is more prevalent, but it too, is mostly about light, pleasant fruit. Cabernet Franc is the red star here and no one builds it better than Charles Joguet of Chinon. These wines are rich and concentrated and very exciting.

The central part of the Loire yields another treasure for me and from the most unlikely grape, the Chenin Blanc. This grape produces real yawners in most of the New World's offerings, but here grown in limestone-clay soils, the wines are austere, honeyed and leafy and with unbelievable aging power.

A number of producers here still have 1947's in the cellars and they have aged very well. If you are lucky enough to find 1989 or 1990 Vouvray or Savennieres from any of the great producers such as Baumard, Poniatowski, Closel, Foreau or Coulee de Serrant, they will age for many delicious years in your cellars.

Around the port of Nantez are vast vineyards of mostly nondescript Muscadet, a dry, light white wine. A few are quite good, most are innocuous, but all accompany nicely the mussels and other shellfish of the region.

On the other side of Paris, Champagne's bizzare deep-chalk soils and cool hills give the world's greatest sparkling wines. Most of the great houses are very trustworthy, so style is more of a consideration than variations of quality. For lighter styles, I like Jacquesson, Deutz, Taittinger, Billecart-Salmon and Moet et Chandon. Mumm, Veuve Clicquot and Pol Roger are excellent weightier styles, while Bollinger, Krug and Roederer have my heart for the bigness and richness they bring to the delicate drink of Champagne.

Abutting Germany, Alsace lies beneath the Vosges Mountains, perilously situated for the last several wars. The wines speak of the twin nationality of the Alsace, the grapes and bottles are Germanic, the wines within are completely French.

Riesling, Pinot Gris, Pinot Blanc and Gewurztraminer are delicious here; crisp, sappy and as rich as any fish dish you can place alongside these wines. I will admit to a preference for German Riesling over most Alsace Riesling however. I am constantly amazed by Riesling's ability to show intense flavor, even at low alcohol levels and that is where Germany steals the march on the French. Typically German Rieslings are less than ten percent alcohol, Alsace Riesling are often as much as thirteen percent.

What is the future for American wine?

For most of the last fifty years, California has been the nation's vineyard. Though many other states are beginning to produce excellent wines, California will remain unchallenged as the leader for many decades to come. Truthfully, California's potential is still unrealized as a producer of a great variety of fine wines and great values.

As noted above, in the last fifteen years regions thought inhospitable to the vine have offered California's most exciting wines, western Sonoma and Green Valley, Anderson Valley, Carneros, Carmel and Santa Barbara are still being explored. Grapes, vine scions and rootstocks, viticultural practices and methods of vinification are being matched to sites where the learning has just begun.

As some of the old practices are being unlearned, so too is California's love affair with the varietal waning. The next ten years will bring more blends of varietals resulting in more generous wines over the life of the wine, more consistent values and greater creative latitude for winemakers.

The bad news is that the new blends are likely to result in greater consumer confusion as the old-fashioned Cabernet and Chenin Blanc are seen alongside Matrimonio and Il Fiasco. As well, a certain homogeneity can result when winemakers can lay aside the idea of making a great Syrah or Zinfandel and try instead to produce a facsimile of a wine that just received a score of 101 points from The Wine Spectator.

What may save us is a stronger and contradictory force. Most winemakers are now keen to select the correct site for their per-ceived 101-point wine and will often allow the site to determine the grapes, the methods and the style of their wine. This is as it should be; the power of the site to place its indelible mark upon a wine is the reason wine can never be turned into a Pepsi. A group of scientists and style designers can't make wine; it's been tried repeatedly. Only the land can give you great wine, and only if you listen and learn every year.

Listening to the land has allowed the winegrowers in Oregon to realize the difficulty of Chardonnay production there and to open themselves up to Pinot Gris, a very promising and tasty wine in the rolling hills of the Willamette Valley. Pinot Noir is still king here, as it deserves to be, and the excellence of the Pinot Noir is belied by the newness of the experiment.

Even in the warm, humid south of Oregon, there's a lot of rea-son to keep considering new options and untried grapes. Merlot and Cabernet have shown well here, and many vines are still untested.

Merlot is certainly king in Washington, where Merlot grown in the Columbia Valley and east, in Walla-Walla, are arguably the best the nation can offer. Certainly for their relative inexperience with the grape (it's only been here fifteen years or so), Washington's winemakers have produced very intense, delicious, chocolate-fla-vored Merlot that can stand alongside any in the country.

I am convinced that Washington's Merlot will lead. And many

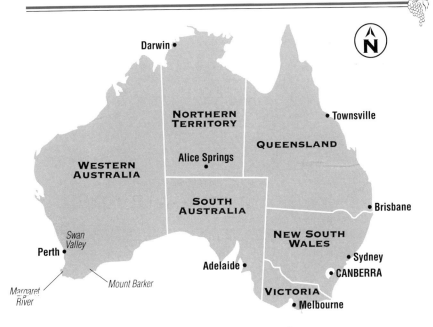

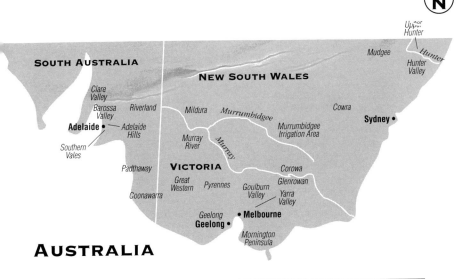

white varietals, chief among them Semillon and Sauvignon Blanc, are first-class.

For the rest of the country, the game's only started. New York has a considerable lead over the others but the learning is happening at a dizzying pace and people in nearly every state of the country will benefit from viticulture's proximity.

Are Australian wines good?

The answer is a resounding yes. Australia's history with the grape is as long as America's and uninterrupted by the stupid "noble experiment" of Prohibition. And not unlike America, Australia's success as a fine wine producer dates from the 50's.

Max Shubert's great Grange Hermitage from Penfolds set the stakes at that time, and has remained one of the world's greatest Shiraz bottles. Shiraz is still the mainstay of Australian red winedom, both at the high and low ends of the spectrum. These wines are delicious by any standards and are well-worth a purchase, whether they are five dollars or fifty.

Cabernets are also quite successful, and are often made tastier by the addition of a touch of Shiraz. Merlots are still nearly uncharted territory and the direction is unclear.

Among whites, Australian Chardonnays are famously fat and oaky and deserve rapid quaffing in their first two years. Other varietals are more or less successful, dependent upon the producer, but Australia is the only maker of Riesling, outside Germany, that offers quality and character.

Do all Italian wines taste the same?

Thankfully, no, but then the world's most diverse wine culture shouldn't suffer from sameness. With over 2000 grapes grown here, there's no reason we can't find some differences.

The landscape is as varied. In the north are the alpine vineyards of the Alto Adige that give way to the warm and sunny Po Valley. Piedmont, the "foot of the hills" described in its name, is a region between the valleys and the mountains and its most famous weather, fog, or *nebbia,* gives the name to the region's greatest grape, Nebbiolo. This grape arguably provides Italy's greatest red wines, Barolo and Barbaresco, and inarguably provides Italy's longest-lived wines.

Italy's better-known grape, Sangiovese, provides its most famous wine, Chianti. The Tuscany district, a beautiful and photogenic region of verdant hills, is home to Chianti's seven subdistricts. In the center, is Chianti Classico, the classic area for Chianti and from which the best wines come. Surrounding Classico are six other Chianti regions; Montalbano, Colli Fiorentini (or, the hills of Florence), Colli Senesi, Colline Pisane, Colli Arentini and Rufina, a small area that can compete with Classico for quality.

These hills provide warmth and sun but shelter cool pockets that, taken together, combine to form an area of exceptional and long growing conditions.

Less dramatically, the Friuli-Venezia, north of Venice, gives much of the same sunny and cool conditions with hills that roll up to the Yugoslavian border. Though reds were traditional here, it is the white wines that vie for the crown as the best in Italy.

Much of Italy then is marked by this contrast of warm hilltops and cool shelter in the hills and mountains. The Appennine chain, running like a spine through Italy gives succor to the winegrower in need of temperate conditions.

As far south as Calabria, the heat of the southern latitude is ameliorated by the cool mountainside vineyards areas. Even Sicily, with its reputation for hot, baked wine, is discovering its cool regions.

The result is a new Italian rennaissance, one already completed with white wines and one beinning for reds. The old, boring, tired whites of ten years ago have been replaced by crisp, clean, focused and food-friendly white wines.

The red wine producers are starting to learn that great things happen when you retain fruitiness in the wine. Many red wines are still produced in the old methods, leaving the grapes to hang until some are dessicated, short hot fermentations, and when the whole

Trentino-
Alto Adige

Fruili-
Venezia
Guilia

Valle
D'Aosta

Lombardy

Veneto

Piedmont

Milan •

Turin •

Asti •

Alba •

Liguria

Emilia-Romagna

Bologna •

• **Venice**

• **Florence**

Tuscany

Marches

• **Montalcino**

Umbria

Latium

Abruzzi

• **Rome**

Molise

Campania

Apulia

Naples •

Sardinia

Basilicata

Calabria

Palermo
•

Sicily

ITALY

thing seems too tannic, aging the wines in barrels until every ves- tige of flavor of fruit is gone. Sounds tasty, huh?

In the next five years, many producers will have gone to clean- er, gentler methods for red wine production, with smaller yields and less barrel time. The result will be an explosion of flavor in Italy and the sameness that existed will be a forgotten joke.

Are South African wines pretty much like the wines from Chile?

That's actually a pretty interesting observation, which one con- sumer afforded me. Both countries are more informed by wine styles of the nineteenth century than they are by the modern, so- called international style. The international style, devised by Emile Peynaud for Bordeaux in the 50's and 60's, came into its own in Bordeaux with the great '82 vintage.

The 1982's were rich, fat, tannic and very low in acid. That made them good drinkers in the first few years and probable can- didates for ten to twenty year aging. Prior to that time, many Bor- deaux combined firm tannins with tart acidity, and the result were wines that could easily age more than twenty-five years, but that were quite unpleasant for much of that time.

Certainly chief among the changes to Bordeaux, manifested in the '82's, was the emphasis upon fruit, thick, rich and delicious. This resulted in wines you could cellar or drink, wines very much at ease on any dinner table.

Some have been critical of the changes; I do not share their opprobrium for Peynaud's style. I think that balance is more important for longevity than tannin and roughness. I am reminded of one of Peynaud's many dictums, "The best way to grow old gracefully is to stay young as long as possible." These wines are sweet and graceful in youth and will be in age.

In Chile, Argentina and South Africa, there is as much opportu- nity for fat and tasty wines as there is in Australia; all very sunny climes. The difference is that the wines those people drink are much more like the old Bordeaux style.

In the last few years, some producers have begun to place

greater emphasis upon fruit and make more commercially viable wines. Most successful are the South Africans, who were already making world-class wines.

South Africa has had over *three hundred years* of uninterrupted wine production to get it right. Now that some producers are claiming fruit as another birthright, many of these wines will begin to find a home in collectors' cellars. Hopefully, they can find a home on the tables as well.

Does anyone drink Sherry or Madeira?

Now, we're going to have to fight because you've just made me mad. I love Sherry and Madeira, as well as the other great man-made fortified, Port. These are some of the world's greatest wines and no one seems to appreciate that anymore.

They all suffer from image problems. The most common drinker of all three is British and the drinker of Sherry is usually some elderly widow, tippling between soap operas. That's an image to excite the yuppie palate. It's not Sherry's fault that little old ladies like it; that doesn't mean that you shouldn't.

Sherry can be produced either dry or sweet, as can Madeira, and the flavors can be exotic and delicious and ought to find new drinkers today. But as Madeira goes through its most difficult time ever (almost 90% of the vineyards need to be replanted), they have little time or money to devote to public relations.

The upshot of this is the Sherry and Madeira have never been, and will never be, cheaper. Find a smart retailer and let them show you what twenty dollars can do for you. Madeira is particularly fun, since an opened bottle, with the cork snugged back in, can last for decades! I keep a selection of ten or so opened at all times in my basement. Mine don't last for more than a year or two, but then, I drink them.

Port is making a strong comeback already, so I think Sherry and Madeira may be awaiting their turn. Good vintage ports from excellent years like 1983 or 1985 are still available at virtually the same prices at which they were released, and ten and twenty-year-old tawny ports are still fairly priced.

While vintage ports are meant to be consumed as soon as you open them, tawnies can last for several months after being cracked open.

FINAL NOTES & DREGS

Nothing succeeds like excess. Most wine books are monumental in scale and scope, the authors seemingly eager to display their knowledge in amazing breadth and detail. I'm not sure where this leaves the average reader, who receives for his or her thirty dollars, a massive tome that could double as furniture.

Obviously that was not the point of this little book. I felt that a true primer would be helpful, one that didn't require a fortnight without sleep to read. In it, I hope I've answered a few questions and illuminated the stuff of wine as me and my friends see it.

The next step for someone on the wine journey is of course to go buy another wine book, and then another. No matter what you read, I hope that any author will always encourage you to taste. Wine is meaningless if you don't drink it.

There is a story that features Robert Parker, perhaps mythically. If it wasn't Parker who said it, I'd like to thank the person who did. The tale goes, that Parker was being accosted by one of the strange wealthy creatures so often drawn to the mystery and fun of wine.

"I have Latour 1990 and 1970 in my basement," the odious braggart boomed. "I've got Pichon-Baron 1989, Pichon Lalande 1970, 1961 and 1959. I've got Margaux '61, Mouton '45, Cheval Blanc '47 and '49, Taylor '45 and '55, Laguiche Le Montrachet, a vertical of Dunn, Conterno Barolo stretching back to the 50's and a cellar full of DRC," he bellowed. "What's the one thing missing from my cellar?"

"A corkscrew," Parker shot back.

If you want to learn about wine, drink. A votre Sante!

Watch for the continuing books on wine & wines with repast, by Doug Frost, and other books published by The Writer's Co.

GLOSSARY

Acidity – the natural grape acids that give a wine its tartness and that provide the structure of white wines. High levels of acidity are responsible for the agebility of certain long-lived white wines, such as those from Germany.

Amarone – an intense full-bodied wine from the Veneto in northern Italy; can be produced in Recioto, or barely sweet styles, or straight Amarone in which all available sugar (and there is plenty) is converted to alcohol.

Amontillado – an delicious, almond-y type of fino, or dry and light, sherry which has received long ageing in barrels; unfortunately, some Amontillado is simply sweetened cheap fino.

A.O.C. – abbreviation for Appellation d'Origine Controlee, indicating the wine comes from a particular place in France and the wine's production has been controlled to some degree by the government.

A.P. number – abbreviation for Anfangsprufungnummer, indicating that the wine has been tested by the German government, and noting the date of bottling.

Aroma – generally described as the smell of the grapes in a wine, as separate from the bouquet which derives from the wine's time in bottle. Could also be understood to be the smell of the wine in total.

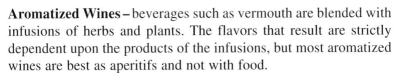

Aromatized Wines – beverages such as vermouth are blended with infusions of herbs and plants. The flavors that result are strictly dependent upon the products of the infusions, but most aromatized wines are best as aperitifs and not with food.

Autolysis – the breakdown of dead yeast cells in a bottle of Champagne, or quality sparkling wine, gives a yeasty, sometimes bready, aroma which grows as the wine sits on the yeast. Great Champagne may age on the yeast, or lees, for five or more years.

Balance – this somewhat esoteric concept describes the interplay of the fruit in the wine, and the structuring elements; tannin and acidity. If the elements are in "balance" the flavors seem harmonious and the wine is likely to live longer than a wine that is out-of-balance, however impressive it might seem. Obviously, harmony is a fairly subjective idea.

Barbaresco – derived from the Nebbiolo grape in Piedmont, can be massive and long-lived.

Barolo – also derived from Nebbiolo in Piedmont, tends to be bigger and more long-lived than its cousin, Barbaresco.

Barrel-Fermented – fermenting white wines in barrel gives a character to the resultant wine of toastiness and spice, often providing flavors of clove, cinnamon and custard. It's interesting to note that a softer oak flavor derives from fermenting wine in oak, than from aging an already fermented wine in oak.

Beaujolais – a region and wine in the southern part of Burgundy in France. The Gamay grape gives a wine of big fruitiness and, usually, short-lived charms, especially in the Nouveau (new wine of a given year) version. Beaujolais Superieur and Villages are just a cut above, although Cru Beaujolais, or Beaujolais from one of the ten best villages (Brouilly, Morgon, Cotes de Brouilly, Regnie, Moulin-a-Vent, Fleurie, Chiroubles, Julienas, Chenas, St. Amour) can be delicious for many years.

Beerenauslese – an intensely sweet German wine, often with impeccable balance and a long life ahead.

Blanc de Blancs – white wine made from white grapes; in Champagne, a wine made only from chardonnay.

Blanc de Noir – a white wine from red grapes (most grape juice is clear, or "white"), in Champagne, a wine made from Pinot Noir and Pinot Meunier.

Body – the body of a wine is chiefly the result of the amount of alcohol in the wine, the more alcohol, the bigger the body.

Bordeaux – the classic region in southwest France where whites are composed of Sauvignon Blanc and Semillon, and reds are blends of Cabernet Sauvignon, Cabernet Franc and/or Merlot, as well as other minor grapes. The area is broken into regions for white wines; among them Graves (dry wines) and Barsac, Cerons or Sauternes (sweet wines), and red wines. The communes of St. Estephe, Pauillac, St. Julien, Margaux, Graves, Haut-Medoc and Medoc are often lumped together as the wines of the Medoc, and are most often Cabernet-based. St. Emilion and Pomerol, as well as their satellites, are more generally Merlot-based. Many regions are classified into standard estates (such as Cru Beaujolais) and Cru Classe', or classified growths. Classed growths are delineated into Premier and Grand Cru Classe', or in 1855 in the Medoc, the first through fifth growths.

Botrytis Cinerea – the Noble Rot, or botrytis cinerea, dessicates grapes and provides the sweet juice of Sauternes and Monbazillac, Germany (Beerenauslese often, Eiswein often, Trockenbeerenauslese always) where it is known as Edelfaule, and other great sweet wines around the world.

Bouquet – generally understood as the smell a wine gains from long bottle-ageing.

Brix – a measurement of the sugar content in a wine.

Brunello di Montalcino – a big and long-lived wine from Tuscany, available in less-expensive, less-oaky and less-long-lived bottling called Rosso di Montalcino

Brut – the standard marque from a sparkling wine or Champagne producer, drier than an "Extra Dry", but sweeter than a "Natural"

Chablis – a Chardonnay from northern Burgundy in France that is generally tart and minerally; it is one of my favorite wines to age. Other bottlings include Petite Chablis which can be good or bad, depending upon the producer, Chablis Premier Cru (from one of the 40 premier vineyards of the area) and Chablis Grand Cru (from one of the seven best vineyards) both of which are likely to be exemplary wines of the region.

Champagne – an area in northern France that produces the world's best sparkling wines, known eponymously as "Champagne".

Charmat – a process in sparkling winemaking in which the secondary fermentation takes place in a large container, not a bottle. Otherwise known as "Cuve Close" and oten seen in inexpensive bubblies from America and Germany.

Chateauneuf-du-Pape – a great red wine from the southern portion of the Rhone Valley in France, composed of Grenache and other regional grapes; it is almost always a good value.

Chianti – a great red wine area in Tuscany producing wines primarily of the Sangiovese grape, a delicious cherry-tasting grape, the area is broken into regions of Montalbano, Colli Fiorentini, Colline Pisane, Rufina, Colli Senesi, or Classico (usually the best).

Claret – the British term for red Bordeaux, can imply a classic and, sometimes, unpretentious wine.

Clone – a lot of talk is given in wine circles to clones, or selections of vinegrapes. Mostly this is geek-speak, but there are quality differences among different clones of the same grape.

Colheita – the Portuguese word for "Vintage"

Cosecha – the Spanish word for "Vintage"

Cote Rotie – a great red wine from the Syrah grape grown on a slope in northern Rhone, France. As expensive as it is, it's a great value.

Cream Sherry – a sweetened Oloroso sherry.

Cremant – the term for non-Champagne sparkling wines in France.

Cru – a growth (an estate) in France, usually denoting a hierarchy, Bourgeois to First growth, or Premier to Grand.

Decanting – pouring the wine into a decanter to aerate it or, more reasonably, seperate the wine from the sediment in the bottom of the bottle.

Demi-Sec – a sweeter style of sparkling wine or Champagne, erroneously translated in America as "Extra Dry".

D.O. – the designation Denominacion de Origen, denotes a wine of a particular place and methods in Spain.

D.O.C. – the abbreviation Denominazione di Origine Controllata in Italy describes a wine of specific grapes from and a specific place and methods. A higher level, DOCG (the "G" is for "Garantita") guarantees that the wine comes one of 13 vineyard areas that have often (but not always) earned higher respect.

Dolcetto – a fruity wine from Piedmont, can be very exciting or can taste like bad Beaujolais.

Eau de Vie – a brandy made of fruit wine

Eiswein – a wine made from frozen grapes, much of the water in the grape stays behind in the form of ice and the resulting wine is more concentrated in grape sugars

Erzaugerabfullung – Generally, an estate-bottled wine in Germany, though the term has been abused.

Estate Bottled – a term designating a wine grown, made and bottled by one producer

Fermentation – the process of converting grape sugars to alcohol and carbon dioxide, through the action of yeasts.

Fino – a light, dry to very dry fortified Sherry wine from Andalusia in Spain

Flor – a yeast growth in fino production in Jerez, Spain and few other regions; the flor protects a fino from air while it is developing in the barrel and imparts flavors.

Fortified Wine – a natural wine blended with some neutral grape spirit or brandy (Port, Sherry, Madeira). The finished wine is roughly 50% higher in alcohol than standard table wine and is often used for dessert.

Garrafeira – a Portuguese term for Reserve

Halbtrocken – a German term for "half-dry", that can be barely dry or semi-sweet

Hermitage – a region of great red wines (Syrah) and white wines (Marsanne and Roussanne) in the northern Rhone. Red Hermitage is always a great value.

Kabinett – a wine of quality in Germany which may be somewhat sweet and may be bone dry; as well, it may be boring and it may be brilliant.

Lees – dead yeast cells found in the bottom of barrels and which can add richness to a wine if the wine is allowed to sit with the lees.

Loire – a large valley in northwestern France, producing Muscadet (very light and very dry), Chinon and Bourgeuil (lovely powerful reds of Cabernet Franc), Vouvray (can be spectacular, long-lived dry to semi-dry white wine from Chenin Blanc) Savennieres (fabulous, bone-dry Chenin Blanc) and Pouilly Fume and Sancerre (most often great, intense Sauvignon Blancs), to name the most common.

Maceration Carbonique – or carbonic maceration as we call it. This process allows the yeast to work in a non-oxygen, or closed, environment which increases fruitiness and lowers acidity. The method is traditional in Beaujolais and with other soft, early-drinking reds.

Macon – a Chardonnay from the southern portion of Burgundy, and can be boring or nearly great, depending upon the producer. The region also makes two relative values, St. Veran and Pouilly Fuisse.

Maderized – as wines break down due to the presence of oxygen, they become maderized, or similar to Madeira, which is a wine intentionally spoiled, if you will. In Europe, this flavor can be sought-after in small proportions and can give an aroma called *rancio*.

Malolactic Fermentation – a secondary fermentation that is common to red wines and utilized to soften the harsh apple-y acids in some white wines. This is not strictly a yeast fermentation, but the result of the presence of a naturally occuring bacteria.

Manzanilla – a incredibly delicate fino-styled Sherry wine from Andalusia. It is rarely seen in top form as it deteriorates in a few months.

Methode Champenoise – the classical method of Champagne production, a secondary fermentation in the bottle in which it is sold. Now known as "Methode Classique".

Mosel – short for "Mosel-Saar-Ruwer", a region of three rivers in Germany producing Germany's most delicate great white wines.

Mousseux – a term for non-Champagne sparkling wines in France, now titled "Cremant".

Muscadet – a very light, very dry white wine from the region of the mouth of the Loire River, begging for shellfish.

Oak – a traditional vessel for wine used by the Romans and in wide use since. If the oak is young, it imparts a substantially oaky flavor to the wine; if older, that impact is greatly lessened.

Oxidation – the process of a wine becoming changed and slowly spoiled by the presence of oxygen, this is why all wine has a lifespan beyond which it is unpleasant to drink.

Palomino – the grape of Sherry, one of the world's most fascinating wines

Phylloxera – a vine-killing louse which wreaked devastation upon the world's vines in the 19th Century, and still causes enormous problems today.

Pierce's Disease – a deadly virus affecting vines throughout California and perhaps farther.

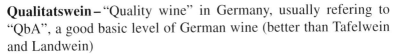

Qualitatswein – "Quality wine" in Germany, usually refering to "QbA", a good basic level of German wine (better than Tafelwein and Landwein)

Qualitatswein mit Pradikat – "Quality wine with distinction", in German usage, this is further broken down into Kabinett, Spatlese, Auslese, Beerenauslese, Eiswein and Trockenbeerenauslese, in order of sugar levels in the unfermented grape juice.

Reserva, Riserva – a term suggesting greater merit and barrel-ageing in wines from Spain, Portugal, Italy, Chile or Argentina.

Reserve – as above, though in American usage, the term has been marketed into absolute non-meaning.

Residual Sugar – the amount of sugar remaining in a bottled wine after fermentation. Most dry wines have less than .5% residual sugar while a sweet could have anywhere from 1.5% to 5%. Some dessert wines have even higher levels of residual sugar, but the character of sweetness is as much determined by the amount of acidity. That is, a 3% residual sugar with very high acidity will taste drier than a wine with 1.5% sugar and no acidity.

Sekt – a sparkling wine from Germany, if "Deutscher Sekt", the wine is made primarily from German grapes.

Solera – a system of fractional blending of different vintages used in Sherry production and a handful of other areas around the world. Many wines, all over the globe, are composed of blends of differing vintages, for quality and economy, though in less elaborate methods than in a true solera.

Spatlese – a German term for grapes with a particular ripeness level, can be dry or sweet

Spumante – sparkling wine in Italy, dry or sweet, though "Asti Spumante" is generally sweet.

Sulfur Dioxide – a natural element used in wine production in trace amounts for stability since the early 1600's.

Suss-reserve – unfermented grape juice used in German wines to add sweetness.

Tannin – the acid found in the skins, stems and seeds of wine grapes (as well as the barrels used to age wines) that gives a dusty character to the wines. Tends to drop out with coloring matter as the wine ages.

Tavel – a great (yes, Virginia) rose from the southern Rhone Valley

Tawny Port – a port which has been aged in barrel its entire life, losing its bright red-purple color and turning orange or tawny.

Tempranillo – one of the great grapes of Rioja in Spain

Trebbiano – a ubiquitous grape in Italy making, usually, innocuous white wine.

Trocken – a term meaning dry, or very low residual sugar in Germany. Some of these trocken wines are rich and tasty, some are a bit bland and warm. Tread carefully.

Trockenbeerenauslese – the "dry berries" suggested in the word are dry from the dessication caused by Edelfaule, or Noble Rot. A very sweet and rare wine.

Ullage – a term used to describe the gradual reduction of the volume of a wine in a bottle as it ages. It naturally shrinks to some degree, though most gross ullage is due to mishandling of the wine.

Varietal – a type of vine and, hence, grape and wine. Wines are either a blend of varietals or labeled as a single varietal (minimum percentages for being labeled as a varietal vary, from America's 75% minimum threshold to Germany's 100%).

V.D.Q.S – an abbreviation for Vins Delimite Qualite Superieure, a level below A.O.C.

Vin de Pays – a French wine "from the country", a level below V.D.Q.S. and A.O.C.

Vinho Verde – a young wine of red or white grapes in Portugal

Vino Nobile di Montepulciano – a wine that can offer value in Tuscany, from a clone of Sangiovese

Vins de Table – ordinary table wine in France

Vintage – the year of a wine's harvest

Vintage Port – a port destined to age in the bottle from a special vintage. Can age from ten to a hundred years.

Vintage Champagne – wine from a good to great vintage in Champagne

Vitis Labrusca – a native species of America, usually undesirable in aroma

Vitis Vinifera – the native European vine providing most of the good and all of the great wines. The vinifera species is further divided into varietals with names such as Chardonnay, Pinot Noir. Cabernet Sauvignon or Syrah.

INDEX

ABOUT THE AUTHOR

Doug Frost is one of only two people *in the world* to hold the celebrated credentials of 'both' Master of Wine *and* Master Sommelier!

Recently Doug was nominated for The James Beard Award for 'Outstanding Beverage Professional of the Year'. Under Doug's wine guidance, The American Restaurant was given the 'DiRona Award' for outstanding achievement, and *The Wine Spectator* 'Best Award of Excellence' for their wine program.

After graduating summa cum laude from Kansas State University in 1977, he began his career in the food and beverage industry, specializing in wine and spirits as buyer and wholesaler.

He is Cellarmaster for Culinary Concepts and Beverage Director for The American Restaurant, where he has created ambitious events such as 'Three Emperor's Dinner' and the 'Great Outdoor Cigar Smoker'!

His wit and personal magnitude is enjoyed by a loyal listening audience on Kansas City's classical music station, KXTR FM, where he is a regular guest.

Doug's beverage column appears monthly in *The Kansas City Star.* Other work has been published in local and national press, such as *Borderline, New Art Examiner* and *Practical Winery & Vineyard.*

Mr. Frost's next book, *Uncorking The Pacific Northwest,* will be published by The Writer's Company later this year.